**Two week
loan**

week loan

ase return or before the last
ped w.
r late return.

European Community Investigations and Sanctions

European Community Investigations and Sanctions

The Supranational Control of Business Delinquency

Christopher Harding

Leicester University Press
Leicester, London and New York

Distributed in the United States and Canada by St Martin's Press

Leicester University Press
(a division of Pinter Publishers)

First published in 1993

Editorial offices
Fielding Johnson Building, University of Leicester,
Leicester, LE1 7RH, England

Trade and other enquiries
25 Floral Street, London, WC2E 9DS *and*
Room 400, 175 Fifth Avenue, New York, NY 10010, USA

Christopher Harding is hereby identified as the author of this work as provided under Section 77 of the Copyright, Designs and Patents Act, 1988.

British Library Cataloguing in Publication Data
A CIP catalogue for this book is available from the British Library

ISBN 0 7185 1384 3

Library of Congress Cataloging-in-Publication Data
A CIP record for this book is available from the Library of Congress

Typeset by Saxon Printing Ltd, Derby
Printed and bound in Great Britain by
Biddles Ltd, Guildford and King's Lynn

Contents

Preface   vi
List of abbreviations   ix
1 Business delinquency and supranational control   1
2 Investigations: procedures and powers   11
3 Investigations: legal control   22
4 Hearings: procedures and rights of defence   41
5 The role of third parties   52
6 Informal settlement   68
7 Sanctions   79
8 Substantive antitrust delinquency in the EEC context   98
9 The national dimension   114
10 Delinquency, criminality and economic regulation   129
Bibliography   145
Index   148

Preface

This work has grown out of some years' reflection on the developing nature of competition law and policy within the European Community. As a subject, competition law has been traditionally the preserve of commercial lawyers and economists, especially in the British literature. In so far as it has been regarded as a legal discipline, its close relations have been identified as the law of contract, of commercial relations, of companies and of intellectual property. These perceived affinities reflect the earlier preoccupation with substantive issues of competition law, centred on the question of when and whether a particular action is unacceptably anti-competitive, which required an exercise of economic analysis within a legal framework of commercial relations. However, with the steady development of both administrative and investigative procedures for the official application of competition policy and law within the European Community, procedural concerns have come increasingly to the fore and legal argument now relates as much to the latter as to substantive issues. In this way the subject has developed new affinities with other legal categories – administrative law, the protection of basic rights and, though this last may come as a surprise, criminal procedure. A reading of contemporary cases on competition matters which reach the European Court of Justice (or more usually now, the Court of First Instance) will reveal as much argument concerning the way in which a case has been handled as that relating to issues of substantive legal and economic analysis.

This book is therefore essentially concerned with the procedures used to enforce the Community's competition policy, but especially with those proceedings which comprise investigations into particular arrangements and the application of sanctions. Although such procedures represent a small part of the activity of implementation in a purely quantitative sense, since a great deal is achieved through administrative and bureaucratic methods, they represent the handling of the most important, difficult and controversial cases and therefore attract a high level of attention. Such proceedings, although in one sense the tip of the iceberg, also represent the development of another dimension of the subject, revealing it more and more as an area of public law with the typical concerns of that field, in terms of the legal relation between official agencies and private individuals. Within the last ten or fifteen years Community competition law has become very much an arena for the judicial review of administrative action, for the assertion of basic rights and for the use of sanctions which, though not criminal in name, may have an appearance and impact similar to that of penalties found in national systems of criminal law.

It is such perceived changes in the juridical character of the subject which have prompted the writing of a monograph dealing with the process of investigation and the implementation of sanctions in the field of Community competition policy. A work of this kind may serve more than one purpose. In the first place, it provides a detailed account of the current state and development of the procedural law in this area, explaining the rules which relate to such matters as the rights of defence of investigated undertakings and the application of fines and other sanctions. There is an ever-increasing body of law on the subject which now deserves attention as a field of study in its own right, against which the questions of substantive law and policy, previously occupying the foreground, serve instead as a backdrop. In addition to such an expository function, there is also an analytical and theoretical exercise now to be performed: to relate the legal phenomenon of Community investigations and sanctions to other legal categories in order to evaluate the operation and development of this area of law. For if the legal control or scrutiny of Community powers and procedures in this context are to be effectively and critically assessed, then the question of their juridical character comes to the fore. In particular, it needs to be asked to what extent such procedures are analogous to criminal proceedings at the national level, especially for purposes of discussing the appropriate level and kind of legal protection for those who are the subject of such legal process.

For the discussion which follows it has therefore been necessary to draw together two areas of law and legal methodology which have hitherto been regarded as largely separate. On the one hand, this is a work about competition law, a subject which has been treated traditionally in an economic and commercial legal context, although with some nods in the direction of public law procedures such as judicial review. But equally, it is a study in criminal justice and the related field of protection of basic rights. The theme of the study being made here concerns the coercive and repressive character of investigations and sanctions, and the legal arguments which have to be considered call to mind the concepts and principles which are to be found in the field of criminal procedure and the rights of defence. It is also an exercise in criminal jurisprudence, testing the limits of appropriate 'criminalisation' in the area of economic regulation and exploring different approaches to law enforcement beyond the traditional scope of national criminal law. The subtitle of the book, 'The Supranational Control of Business Delinquency', is intended to convey both the essential substance of the discussion and the viii

conceptual ambiguity in the system of control which has been developed at the Community level in relation to competition questions.

The ideas which have fed into this discussion have been developed and reworked over a considerable period of time and I therefore have to acknowledge a general debt to those many people who have enabled me at different times to test my theories. I have drawn a great advantage from the exposure to European, as distinct from British ways of looking at this kind of subject, particularly through discussion with members of the Willem Pompe Instituut at the University of Utrecht. Although they may not be aware of it, both Ann Sherlock of the Aberystwyth Law Faculty and René Guldenmund of the Department of Criminal Law at Utrecht have stimulated and corrected my thinking on the subject. As with much work which is long in gestation, it may however prove to be short in the writing and I need also to thank my family for their indulgence towards phases of abstraction or unsociability that I have no doubt been prone to in recent months. The indulgence that I hope may be shown by readers is the acknowledgement that there is much more which could be said on this subject, and no doubt will be said, and that what follows should be seen in the nature of a signpost for such future work.

C. H.
Aberystwyth, May 1992.

List of abbreviations

The following abbreviations are commonly used in footnote references. Most references are to English language sources.

C. M. L. R.	Common Market Law Reports
C. M. L. Rev.	Common Market Law Review
E. C. L. R.	European Competition Law Review
E. C. R.	European Court Reports
E. H. R. Rep.	European Human Rights Reports
E. L. Rev.	European Law Review
H. L.	House of Lords
J. O.	Journal Officiel (pre- 1972 French language version)
O. J.	Official Journal of the European Communities

1 Business delinquency and supranational control

On 21 December 1989 the European Communities Commission adopted a decision condemning the activities of a number of major companies involved in the European petrochemical industry.[1] These companies had engaged in collusion, secretly agreeing to restrict competition between themselves as regards the supply of the thermoplastic product, PVC, important for its use in a number of industrial contexts, such as heavy industry and construction, and in a number of consumer applications. In the words of the Commission, these companies had:

> deliberately set up and operated a secret and institutionalised system of regular meetings to fix prices and volume targets in an important industrial product. Several of the undertakings concerned ... had already been the subject of fines imposed by the Commission for collusion in the chemical industry.[2]

This policy adopted by the cartel of PVC manufacturers was identified by the Commission as a concerted practice, prohibited by Article 85(1) of the EEC Treaty. As well as requiring the companies to bring their restrictive practice to an end, the Commission imposed fines totalling 37 million ECU on the cartel members, who subsequently lodged complex legal arguments of appeal against this decision with the European Court of First Instance. The latter, discovering procedural defects in the Commission's procedure, overturned the decision in February 1992, prompting the Commission to appeal in turn to the European Court of Justice.[3]

The case of the PVC Cartel, which in its successive legal stages has been running for a number of years, is just one example (if quite a dramatic one) of a kind of proceeding which has become increasingly common during the 1970s, 1980s and 1990s, and is concerned with the control of the market behaviour of companies or 'undertakings', as such parties are often termed at the European level. On the face of it, the proceeding described above appears very much like the prosecution and punishment of offending conduct which is the staple diet of national systems of criminal law. There are, however, a number of significant legal differences. In the first place, such a procedure is not part of a national legal system, but is operated under the European Community legal order, which is juridically distinct from, though also closely related to the legal structures of the Community Member States. Nor was liability established and sentence passed by a court of law, but by part of the main executive organ of an international organisation. Finally, the entire procedure used in such cases may not officially be termed a criminal proceeding. For want of a better term it is usually described as an 'administrative procedure'. In substantive terms, however, it may be fairly described as the supranational control of business delinquency. Is it therefore a novel and radically different legal phenomenon? Or is it a familiar legal process dressed up in different terminology? The following discussion seeks to provide some kind of answer to these questions.

The legal dilemma at the heart of this discussion was succinctly stated by Advocate General Vesterdorf of the European Court of First Instance in a recent case[4] relating to another EEC competition proceeding also concerned with the prosecution of a major international cartel alleged to have violated Article 85 of the Treaty, this time in connection with another thermoplastic product, polypropylene. Significantly enough some of the same companies were involved again and here too they presented an impressive battery of legal argument against the Commission decision taken against them. As will become clear as the discussion unfolds, many of the these arguments depend ultimately on the juridical characterisation of these competition proceedings. The Advocate General described the problem in the following terms:

> This question touches upon one of the major difficulties which arises in the handling of competition cases ... the tension which can clearly be felt ... between the procedural framework of the cases, consisting of an administrative procedure followed by judicial review of legality, and the substance of the cases, which all broadly exhibit the characteristics of a criminal law case. In many instances the parties' submissions can only be understood with the help of the terminology and concepts in criminal law and procedure.[5]

The underlying question is therefore whether what is at issue here is properly analysed as a form of criminal law, with the legal consequences in terms of such matters as procedure, rights of defence and enforcement which would follow from such an analysis, or as something juridically different, either borrowing from other analogies at the national level (such as 'administrative procedure') or something generically novel. Clearly this question may only be answered on the basis of a close examination of the various elements of the Community's competition procedure, from the earliest phases of investigation through to the final stages of enforcement of sanctions. Before doing so, something should be said about three of the principal concepts which inform much of this discussion and this first chapter will therefore explore further the ideas of supranational control, business delinquency and criminal and administrative proceedings.

Supranational control

The development of the European Economic Community has been a mould-breaking process as regards a number of aspects of international organisation and cooperation. The degree of economic integration achieved by the sovereign States which are members of the Community and more recent moves towards integration in the social and political spheres by the Community countries have been exceptional in an international community which, though increasingly interdependent in many respects, is still formally dominated by the dogma of State sovereignty and independence.[6] The transfer of sovereign powers to the Community institutions goes far beyond what has been achieved in other programmes of international cooperation and over a period of thirty or so years has taken the Community nearer to the models of confederal and federal organisation. Much of this development has been evolutionary and it is easy enough to identify stages of progress and milestones in organisational change:[7] from the limited scope of cooperation in the earliest Community, that concerned with coal and steel, through the establishment of the more widely-ranging Economic Community at the end of the 1950s, its political maturing and democratisation in the 1970s, its developing interest in the social and environmental spheres during the 1980s, to the realisation of monetary union and tentative alignment of national foreign policy in the early 1990s. While these developments have been gradual – and in some respects both tentative and uncertain – the very element of compromise which has so characterised the emergence of Community policy has no doubt also been a reason for its increasingly irreversible achievement. However, such pragmatic and essentially negotiated foundations have also led to a juridical ambiguity in the Community's legal and organisational structure. The European Court of Justice was quick to point out the distinctive nature of the Community's system of rules (*sui generis*),[8] inhabiting an uncertain region between the familiar categories of public international law and national federal law. There has been some academic speculation as to the nature of the emerging Community legal order: whether it was most akin to a federal model,[9] or simply an unusual regional species of international law.[10] One thing remains certain. It is difficult to categorise it neatly as either a political or legal phenomenon and this uncertainty of identity infects a number of its more specific areas of operation.

One particularly distinctive feature of the Community resides in the fact that it is (legally) an international organisation which (very unusually) in some of its areas of competence has immediate responsibility for ensuring the enforcement of its own policies. The standard model for international cooperation is for intergovernmental agreement which is implemented largely through national agencies who may be accountable either indirectly via their governments' international responsibility or more ambitiously in some way to a common (international) institution charged with surveillance. In short, the achievement of policy agreed at the international level is usually delegated to national mechanisms of execution, with any failure to implement what is agreed to be taken up at the international level. In many areas of international cooperation such an approach is sufficient since what is being regulated is governmental behaviour and the traditional processes of international law are appropriate for that purpose. But it is part of the incursive character of Community economic regulation that it is concerned necessarily with the activities of individuals as much as that of governments or their agencies. In some areas of Community policy the regulation of individual commercial activity has again been delegated to national agencies of enforcement through the legal device of making some Community law directly applicable (that is, law to be applied alongside national law) and directly effective (capable of being invoked before national courts).[11] This method is used for example in relation to the important area of Community agricultural policy, in which a large number of rapidly changing and detailed Community rules are given effect by relevant national bodies, such as the Intervention Board for Agricultural Produce in the U.K., with the Community adopting just a supervisory role through the possibility of legal questions being referred to the European Court of Justice.[12]

In some areas of policy, however, the Community has itself taken on a major role of implementation and enforcement. The most notable example is in relation to competition policy under the EEC Treaty. In this area the Community itself has dealt directly with individual market participants, examining their practices, carrying out investigations, handing down individual decisions of approval or condemnation and, in a minority of cases, applying sanctions. There are some similar arrangements under the more specialised Coal and Steel Community Treaty, and likewise some provision of this kind has been made in relation to the regulation of transport under the EEC Treaty.[13] But the EEC regulation of competition is by far the most significant area of direct intervention, because of both its wide scope and the number of cases to be dealt with, and the nature of the sanctions which may be applied; and in both the cases of coal and steel and transport often what is being directly regulated is competition in those specific sectors. It is therefore the implementation of competition policy which has emerged as the most appropriate subject for centralised as distinct from delegated enforcement. This may be largely explained by the fact that, for the policy itself to be worked out at the Community level, the Community required a direct experience of assessing individual cases of anti-competitive behaviour.[14] Such a case-by-case evolution of policy dependent upon first-hand experience therefore suggested that the Community's principal executive organ, the Commission, undertake for itself the examination and assessment of restrictive business practices which injured competition at the Community level. Moreover, the fact that such assessment was to be made in relation to the impact on competition in the Community context provided a further reason for believing that national agencies of control, applying a narrower national perspective, could not so well be entrusted with the task.

The exigencies of Community competition policy in particular, therefore, have led to a situation of international or 'supranational' control of individual business behaviour. The term 'supranational' may be preferable in this context. 'International' is suggestive of inter-governmental relations and accountability and may be more appropriately reserved for such areas of activity as the international protection of human rights or surveillance by a body such as the International Atomic Energy Agency.[15] To a very large extent the behaviour of individuals, whether natural or corporate persons, is within the province of State sovereignty and therefore of national legal systems. Investigation and control of individuals and companies by a body such as the European Communities Commission is therefore a reaching down from the international to the national level which is legally distinctive but essentially represents a system of control which takes place at a level above that of national law, hence *supra*national. But this supranational characterisation is itself productive of a number of legal problems on account of its juridical ambiguity. As noted in the above statement by Advocate General Vesterdorf, the methods used to carry out investigation and enforcement are very much reminiscent of the kind of procedures found in national legal systems, and so in legal argument such analogies are inevitably put forward. Yet the Commission is not a national agency, operating and accountable under national law. It is a Community body, a creature of the Community legal order and accountable to other Community institutions, notably the European Court of Justice. As will be seen from the discussion which follows, this ambiguous position, spanning two kinds of legal system, gives rise to distinctive problems, which may not be wholly novel, since they suggest elements of both the federal and the international, but cannot be resolved easily by reference to one or other of these models of legal organisation.

Business delinquency

It would be helpful at this point to provide in very general terms some legal profile of this direct intervention which is carried out by the Commission in the field of competition policy. To borrow terms from the national legal context, it is able to employ procedures which are suggestive of both the 'administrative' and the 'criminal'. One of the Commission's main functions in the area of competition policy is to assess the compatibility of different kinds of commercial practice with the fundamental requirements of competition protection as embodied in Articles 85 and 86 of the EEC Treaty.[16] Much of this work can be done in a routine, bureaucratic way which may be described as 'administrative'. Under the main implementing Regulation in the competition field, Council Regulation 17 of 1962, a procedure[17] is laid down whereby agreements and practices may be notified by the parties involved to the Commission for the latter's examination. In quantitative terms, the bulk of competition law and practice at the Community level is implemented through this mechanism of notification.[18] At the same time the Commission cannot realistically expect full compliance with the process of notification. It is not in any case a matter of legal obligation to notify, although the risks of operating an anti-competitive practice in breach of Articles 85 and 86 without notification are legally serious.[19] Yet there will inevitably be a certain number of companies which, while aware of the possibility of infringing the Community rules, will be tempted by the potential profit involved in some restrictive practices to go ahead with such activities despite the attempts at regulation by bodies such as the Commission. It is at this point that it becomes appropriate to talk in terms of commercial delinquency.

The deliberate and purposeful, though often covert challenge of competition policy by economically significant market participants is an undoubted problem of both national and international economic regulation. Sufficient examples will emerge from the ensuing discussion to clarify the kind of conduct which is referred to here, but it is typified by classic antitrust violators such as price fixing and market sharing cartels which have in the past thrived in the market conditions of North America and Western Europe. There is a clear consensus within liberal capitalism that such market behaviour represents a private accumulation of economic power which is generally contrary to the public interest and especially injurious to the position of smaller traders and of consumers. In the United States at the end of the nineteenth century, the condemnation of 'antitrust' violations in legislation went so far as to classify such behaviour as criminal with offences being punishable by prison sentences.[20] While most other national legal systems have not proceeded so far along that particular path, a number have adopted repressive measures of control, making use of sanctions such as legal nullity and financial penalties. The concept of business delinquency is thus being employed in the present context to indicate a contumacious attitude towards attempts at the regulation of competition which are designed to promote fairness of economic opportunity. Given its deliberate but often furtive nature, such delinquency, if it is to be controlled, must be subject to procedures of investigation and sanctioning which, in terms of legal analysis, suggest the methodology of criminal proceedings at the national legal level.

While the original Community Member States were willing to grant the Commission such powers of investigation and the ability to impose sanctions in Council Regulation 17, this was clearly on the understanding that this did not involve a transfer of sovereign power in the field of criminal law.[21] This was a subject of considerable political sensitivity. Criminal law in particular was (and remains) an exercise of State activity which is jealously guarded by most governments as being within an area of untouchable sovereignty. It is one thing to transfer sovereign power to an international institution in relation to matters of economic policy and regulation; quite another, in the view of most governments, to hand over any of the symbolically significant machinery of criminal procedure. For this reason, the Commission's procedures of direct intervention in the field of competition policy, comprising significant powers of investigation and the imposition of sanctions, have often been described as 'administrative', while Article 15(4) of the Regulation states specifically that the fines provided for in that Article are not of a criminal law nature. This is important rhetoric, since it reveals an awareness of the political and legal steps which were being taken towards establishing a system of supranational control. At the same time the radical nature of that development was being tempered by the formal qualification of its character. These procedures may look like criminal proceedings to the untrained eye, but this is not the official intention.

'Criminal' and 'administrative' procedures

At a number of points in this discussion arguments will be presented which turn upon the distinction between 'criminal' and 'administrative' procedures and sanctions. The significance of the distinction in legal terms derives from the social consequences of labelling conduct as 'criminal', resulting firstly in a stigmatisation of the offender and requiring then as a result a sufficient degree of legal protection for those who are subjected to procedures which may lead to such an outcome. This requirement of legal protection – a guarantee of adequate rights of defence in relation to a procedure with potentially serious consequences – is reflected in instruments such as the European Convention on Human Rights, which in Article 6 seeks to ensure fair treatment for those subject to criminal proceedings. The advantages of an 'administrative' procedure are generally perceived as residing in greater informality and flexibility and a lower public visibility, reducing the level of stigmatisation and so arguably minimising the alienation of the offending party. The other result of using an administrative procedure is that, being by its nature less legalistic, defence rights are seen as less vital. It will be seen, for instance, that in the context of Community competition proceedings it has been argued on a number of occasions that the level of legal protection for defending parties guaranteed under the European Convention should not be imported since the procedure in question is 'administrative' rather than 'criminal'.[22]

On the other hand, the seriousness of the conduct being investigated in these competition proceedings and the incursive and sometimes coercive nature of the investigation itself, coupled with the repressive quality of some of the sanctions which are applied, are highly suggestive of the criminal proceeding model. During the 1980s an increasing number of appeals to the European Court of Justice have sought to press this analogy so as to import a greater element of legal scrutiny over the way in which competition proceedings are conducted, and the Court's response to this legal challenge forms the subject of a good part of the discussion in this book. In this respect the Court has had to choose between, on the one hand, an adherence to one or other of these models as derived from the national context, and, on the other hand, building upon the distinctive nature of the Commission's powers of control. The ambiguous position of the Community's system of intervention, formally denied the characterisation of criminal procedure and operating at a supranational level, has complicated its task but also allowed it the scope to discover a fresh basis for its solutions.

Plan of discussion

The plan of discussion is therefore organised very much around the tension generated by these conflicting legal arguments. It is necessary in the first place to provide some outline and description of the Commission's powers of investigation and sanction, while at the same time indicating the legal arguments which have been brought before the Court of Justice, and more recently the Court of First Instance,[23] in order to qualify the exercise of these powers. Chapter 2 therefore outlines the basic powers of investigation while Chapter 3 discusses the elements of legal control which have been developed so far in relation to this first stage of the Commission's procedure. If it is decided, on the basis of investigation, to move towards a formal decision against the parties concerned, imperatives of justice require some kind of hearing – an opportunity for the defending parties to put forward their own case. Chapter 4 outlines the procedure laid down for such hearings. Already in this organisation of the discussion it is tempting to perceive some analogies with the familiar stages of criminal proceeding – prosecution, trial, and conviction, to be followed by sentence. Yet it also becomes clear that the Commission's procedure, both in its original concept and in the way in which it has been developed in practice, cannot be fitted into such a scheme so neatly. The possibility of a negotiated outcome (more suggestive of an administrative process) remains strong and the role of third party complainants has a significance which is unlikely to be found in the context of most criminal proceedings. It is necessary therefore to analyse also the impact of both third party involvement and informal settlement in order to gain a full juridical picture, and Chapters 5 and 6 deal respectively with these topics. Chapter 7 then considers the important issue of sanctions and much of the discussion there inevitably deals with the substantial practice and case law which has now developed in relation to the use of fines. At that point it is also helpful to examine the substantive nature of the conduct which is actually subject to these repressive measures in order to identify the kernel of the 'competition offence' and the main elements of liability in relation to fines. Chapter 8 is thus an attempt to delineate the concept of 'antitrust delinquency'. A further dimension of the Commission's procedure concerns those points that interrelate with national rules, given the parallel application of Community and national rules within the same geographical area and the necessary involvement of Member State agencies with some aspects of the Commission's enforcement activity. These questions are dealt with in Chapter 9, along with the issue of extra-territorial enforcement beyond the geographical boundaries of the EEC. On the basis of this discussion, Chapter 10 then attempts to reach some conclusion concerning the juridical character of the Commission's competition procedure.

Notes

1 O.J. 1989, L74/1.
2 Ibid., L74/17.
3 Cases T-79/89, T-84-86/89, T-89/89, T-91-92/89, T-94/89, T-96/89, T-98/89, T-102/89 and T-104/89, *Re the PVC Cartel: BASF and others v Commission* (1992) 4 C.M.L.R. 357.
4 Case T-7/89, *Re the Polypropylene Cartel, Hercules Chemicals v Commission* (1992) 4 C.M.L.R. 84.
5 Ibid., at p. 100.
6 This rhetoric is clearly expressed in a number of the provisions of the United Nations Charter and other instruments, especially General Assembly Resolutions, emanating from the United Nations.
7 See, for example, D. Lasok and J.W. Bridge, *Law and Institutions of the European Communities* (5th ed., 1991, Butterworths), Ch 1, for a general overview of the development of the European Communities.
8 Case 26/62, *Van Gend en Loos v Nederlandse Tariefcommissie* (1963) E.C.R. 1.
9 See, for example, Peter Hay, 'The Federal Jurisdiction of the Common Market Court', 12 (1963) *American Journal of Comparative Law* 39.
10 Derek Wyatt, 'New Legal Order or Old?', 7 (1982) E.L.Rev. 147.
11 See T.C. Hartley, *The Foundations of European Community Law* (2nd ed., 1988, Oxford University Press), Ch. 7, on direct effect and direct applicability.
12 Under Article 177 of the EEC Treaty which enables Member State courts to refer to the European Court of Justice questions concerning either the interpretation or validity of Community measures; see Hartley, op. cit., Ch. 9.
13 See Chapter 10 in this volume, below, for further discussion of Commission procedures in these special sectors.
14 The reasons for this are more fully explored by Ian Forrester and Christopher Norall, 'The Laicization of Community Law: Self-Help and the Rule of Reason – How Competition Law is and could be Applied', 21 (1984) C.M.L.Rev. 11.
15 International Atomic Energy Agency inspections are usually carried out under the Treaty for the Non-Proliferation of Nuclear Weapons of 1970.
16 See Appendix 1 of Christopher Bellamy and Graham Child, Common Market Law of Competition (3rd ed., 1987, Sweet & Maxwell), for the texts of Article 85 and 86 of the EEC Treaty.
17 See Articles 2, 4 and 5 of Regulation 17.
18 The process of notification is considered further in Chapter 2 in this volume.
19 See Bellamy and Child, *op. cit*, Ch 11.
20 On the development of U.S. Antitrust law, see E. Thomas Sullivan (ed.), *The Political Economy of the Sherman Act: The First 100 Years* (1991, Oxford University Press).

21 Some of the original Member States raised constitutional objections to any transfer of powers in relation to criminal law.

22 See in particular the discussion in Chapter 3 in this volume.

23 The Court of First Instance took over the jurisdiction in competition appeals (appeals against the legality of Commission decisions under Articles 85 and 86 of the EEC Treaty, and against fines) in September 1989; see decision of the Council, 24 October 1988, establishing the Court of First Instance, O.J. 1988, L 319/1.

2 Investigations: procedures and powers

In both a quantitative and a qualitative sense the Commission's powers of investigation are undoubtedly of greatest significance in the field of competition policy. A vast number of anti-competitive activities are potentially within the purview of the Commission and its role in the competition field has presented a special challenge both in terms of managing limited resources and developing experience and expertise. The Commission's powers of investigation are defined in Council Regulation 17 of 1962,[1] which came into force on 13 March 1962. Prior to the adoption of this measure, Article 89 of the EEC Treaty provided in the interim for the Commission to investigate suspected anti-competitive acts 'in cooperation with the competent authorities of the Member States' and to authorise those authorities to take measures necessary to remedy the situation. The role of national authorities was not subsequently excluded altogether under Regulation 17: they may retain enforcement functions so long as the Commission has not itself 'initiated a procedure' (Article 9(3) of the Regulation) and they may also be associated in Commission investigations, as discussed below. In practical terms, however, the enforcement of EEC competition policy has remained very much in the hands of the Commission. While in some respects this may be viewed as a notable development of 'supranational' executive power, it may also be argued that this state of affairs reduces the effectiveness of enforcement, since in practice the Commission does not and cannot hope to have sufficient resources to monitor every aspect of the implementation of competition policy; and the absence as yet of a vigorous system of parallel enforcement through private litigation, as has developed in the United States,[2] may well leave a large amount of anti-competitive behaviour in the dark.

Within the Commission, enforcement of competition policy has been the responsibility of Directorate General IV (DG IV), which has a total executive staff of around 150 officials. The internal organisation of DG IV was changed at the beginning of 1984. Prior to that date there had been a clearer division of procedural responsibilities: inspections, studies and investigations had been carried out by Directorate A, but the investigation team from Directorate A did not see a case through to the end but would hand it on to colleagues in Directorate B (restrictive practices), or Directorate C (mergers, coal and steel questions, transport, energy and industrial property rights) for any hearing or decision. However, the reform of 1984 made Directorates B, C and D responsible for dealing with restrictive practices and dominant positions in different industrial sectors (for instance, Directorate B deals with electrical goods, Directorate C with raw chemical products) and within its relevant sector each Directorate is now responsible for all stages of a case.[3] There is also within the Commission a legal service, which is independent of the Directorates General and will necessarily be involved in providing advice in such matters as competition proceedings.

Viewed from the outside, the Commission's share of responsibility for competition proceedings may be open to criticism: it acts as investigator, prosecutor, judge and sentencer in each case, controlled only through the right of appeal against formal decisions to the European Court of Justice. Moreover, the earlier distinction between investigation and prosecution has now been removed.[4] But it would be misleading to take away an impression of the Commission as a monolithic institution. Rather, in the same way as the French administration is a judge of its own behaviour under the French system of administrative law (and is considered by many commentators to operate effectively as such),[5] the Commission has its own internal system of scrutiny, or checks and balances, with of course the further possibility of review by the Court of Justice. Simply dividing the responsibility for investigations and other parts of the procedure may not in itself provide a guarantee of mutual scrutiny. More emphasis should be placed for this purpose on the existence of the Commission's legal service which represents the Commission as a whole in any proceedings before the Court of Justice and in this role will naturally wish to anticipate any legal problems and is likely to alert the relevant officials to any legally doubtful practice.

Nor is the combination of 'pre-trial', 'trial' and 'sentencing' functions wholly unknown at the national legal level. Certainly decisions relating to liability and sentence may often be taken by the same body (in English criminal procedure, to give just one example) and the idea of a specialised or 'expert' sentencing body has sometimes been viewed with considerable misgiving.[6] As regards the combination of prosecutorial and trial functions, in some European systems (France and Italy, for example) these are treated as two types of judicial responsibility within the same court jurisdiction. Similarly, within the Commission's procedure there is a separation of personnel for such purposes. In practice, each case is assigned to a team but is effectively steered by one member who will draft reports on the case and initiate the successive stages of the proceeding. Although by no means individually as powerful or as independent as the 'investigating magistrate' or *juge d'instruction*, this Commission *rapporteur* prepares a case and compiles a dossier in a similar way, perhaps with a greater degree of accountability to immediate colleagues, to superiors and to the Commission's legal service. Formal decisions, such as are provided for at various points in the procedure under Regulation 17, are very much collective in nature. Indeed, these were originally decisions taken by the Commission as a whole, but since 1980[7] certain decision-making powers have been delegated to the Commissioner for Competition (for instance, the decision ordering an investigation under Article 14(3) of the Regulation). Such delegation has not passed unquestioned. In one case,[8] the delegation of the signing of a statement of objections from the Commissioner for Competition to the Head of DG 1V was impugned before the Court of Justice, but approved by the latter in its judgement. This does, however, serve to underline the importance of the principle of collective responsibility with its implicit element of internal control, as regards the more significant formal acts of the Commission in this field.

The legality of the combination of prosecutorial and trial functions within the Commission was also raised before the Court of Justice in the early 1980s,[9] when it was argued that this amounted to a breach of Article 6 of the European Convention on Human Rights. Both Advocate General Slynn and the Court[10] responded to that argument by saying that the Commission cannot be regarded as a 'tribunal' within the meaning of Article 6, and dealt with the general thrust of the complainant's argument by asserting that the Commission's procedure did ensure the right to a fair hearing. This response by the Court is, however, short and evasive, skirting around the basic objection and provides just one example of a reliance on labels such as 'administrative' (as distinct from 'judicial'). The more convincing answer, it will be suggested, is one based on the reality of the system of checks within the Commission's own internal organisation.

Notice of suspected infringements

There are a number of ways in which a suspected infringement of the competition rules may be brought to the Commission's notice: voluntary notification by the parties to a restrictive practice; complaint by a third party; incidental notice, for instance through discussion with Member State authorities, or following questions in the European Parliament; or through a systematic investigation of a particular sector of the market.

Notification is an important procedure whereby many arrangements are made known to the Commission; it is a lynchpin of the EEC competition procedure, but will be considered only briefly here since the topic is covered in detail elsewhere.[11] From the earliest days, market participants have been encouraged to notify any potentially anti-competitive practice to the Commission. Notification not only provides the Commission with information but has also allowed it over the years to gather in the raw material for developing its expertise. In other words, it has provided the means for the development of policy through a case-by-case consideration of different types of commercial arrangement. Voluntary notification has been encouraged by offering substantial carrots – immunity from any fine and an interim guarantee of the enforceability of the agreement in question ('provisional validity').[12] The specific purpose of notification, and the parties' hope, is that their arrangement will either be cleared (approved as not being significantly or at all anti-competitive: a 'negative clearance') or exempted under the conditons laid down in Article 85(3) of the EEC Treaty (anti-competitive in appearance, but allowed to operate because it confers important commercial benefits). Since Regulation 17 came into force, the number of notifications has become enormous and in practice the Commission has selected particular cases which present significant, unusual or controversial features, for full examination. Many notified agreements are dealt with informally or eventually fall within the scope of 'group' or 'block' exemptions under Article 85(3), which provide a blanket approval for certain closely defined common types of commercial arrangement. Although, therefore, notification is an important procedure in quantitative and practical terms, it will only very occasionally lead to a full-scale investigation and formal decision.

Complaints are a more significant trigger for a Commission investigation and the number of complaints has increased over the years.[13] In official terms, a complaint is an 'application' made under Article 3 of Regulation 17. It may be presented either by a Member State or by any 'natural or legal person' with a 'legitimate interest'. Member State governments do not have to show any special interest, although in this context they would be likely to be acting on behalf of individual traders in their own countries. For instance, in the mid-1970s four Member State governments complained about the activities of of a French trading association, UISF, which had adopted restrictive measures in relation to seed imports from other Community countries.[14] The 'legitimate interest' of individual complainants has never been defined either by the Commission or the Court of Justice, in general terms, but may be understood from a number of examples. Typically complaints are received from traders or consumers whose interests are adversely affected by the allegedly anti-competitive act, but representative bodies such as trade unions may also be credible complainants[15] (the role of complainants is discussed more fully in Chapter 5).

In practice the Commission is flexible in its response to complaints. No particular form is required although naturally a written complaint is preferred and a Form C is available for the filing of complaints. The Commission may even act upon an anonymous complaint, which may lead to an investigation on its own initiative. Written complaints are obviously important for the purpose of establishing evidence and for any formal participation by the complainant in the ensuing procedure.

The policy of the Commission is to consider all complaints (although it does not consider itself bound to consider those that are anonymous), initially with a view to establishing whether they are well-founded. If at this stage the

Commission is minded to reject the complaint, it must first of all, under Article 6 of Regulation 99 of 1963, supply the complainant with a provisional notice to this effect, stating its reasons, and must allow the complainant to submit further comments in writing. When a complaint is finally rejected the Commission is not strictly bound by any Community legislation to do so in a formal decision, but this is Commission practice and there is now a view that not to do so would infringe upon the requirements of good administrative practice.[16] A formal rejection of the complaint may also be embodied in a later decision addressed to the subject of the complaint but favourable to such party.[17] Any such decision may well be open to challenge by the original complainant before the Court of Justice, under Article 173 of the EEC Treaty as a party 'directly and individually concerned' by the decision.[18] The complaints procedure is therefore in itself a significant administrative proceeding subject to legal regulation and review.

As regards incidental methods of discovering possible infringements of the competition rules, generalisation is clearly not possible and there is no scope, by the very nature of the situation, for any standard or formal procedure. But in order to illustrate briefly the kind of problems which may arise in this context, some reference should be made to the Stanley Adams case in the 1970s. Adams was a senior marketing executive of the Swiss pharmaceutical company Hoffmann-la Roche. He decided to leave the company's employment: he was deeply disillusioned with the company's 'arrogant' commercial policies and for that reason wrote to the Commissioner for Competition, providing information about its anti-competitive practices within the EEC. He subsequently provided further oral and documentary evidence to the Commission, on the basis of which legal proceedings were taken against the company. The Commission later unintentionally, but with some degree of carelessness, allowed the Swiss authorities to work out Adams' identity as the 'whistle blower', and he was prosecuted in Switzerland for industrial espionage, with distressing consequences for himself and his family.[19] Leaving aside for the moment the legal issues arising from this case, it can be appreciated that there may arise difficult questions of confidentiality in relation to such disclosures. Many sources of information for the Commission may be straightforward, but the Adams case warns of some of the possible legal and personal pitfalls.

The fourth way in which the Commission may be alerted to particular anti-competitive activities is through 'sector enquiries'. These come about through a more general observation of market conditions: economic facts speaking for themselves rather than individual reporting. The power to carry out such an enquiry is conferred by Article 12(1) of Regulation 17:

> If in any sector of the economy the trend of trade between Member States, price movements, inflexibility of prices or other circumstances suggest that in the economic sector concerned competition is being restricted or distorted within the common market, the Commission may decide to conduct a general inquiry into

that economic sector and in the course thereof may request undertakings in the sector concerned to supply the information necessary for giving effect to the principles formulated in Articles 85 and 86 of the Treaty and for carrying out the duties entrusted to the Commission.

In practice the Commission has made relatively little use of these powers, but inquiries were carried out, for instance, in the 1960s into the margarine and brewery sectors and in the 1970s into the oil sector.

Formal investigation

Once the Commission has been alerted to the possible existence of an anti-competitive practice, the preparation of its case may take some considerable time. Although information may have been provided through notification or by complainants or informants, this may be insufficient to construct a convincing case against the party or parties in question. There is often a need for further evidence or for verification of information already supplied. This was clearly contemplated in the drafting of Regulation 17 since two of its provisions allow for further investigatory action – requests for information (Article 11), and inspections or investigations (Article 14). A formal investigation is unlikely to follow from notification, where an informal contact is usually maintained and this may lead to requests for clarification. Such an informal procedure follows from the voluntary nature of the notification and is therefore perhaps better categorised as a species of negotiation rather than prosecution, especially in the majority of cases which result in an informal settlement.

Requests for information

The Commission's power to make such requests is laid down in Article 11(1). This is a potentially wide power which can be used not only in relation to persons suspected of infringements, but also Member State governments and authorities, and other private parties ('undertakings'). Complainants and competitors may be asked to supply information, in particular to enable the Commission to collect the data necessary for market analysis. The information requested must be 'necessary' for the general purposes of enforcing the rules on competition. This raises the question of whether the Commission can embark on a 'fishing expedition'; that is, does the information have to be strictly relevant to the alleged anti-competitive conduct under investigation, or is it permissible to trawl for wider evidence which may relate to other possible breaches? This is a question which begs some difficult issues of necessity, but in the Community context it may be safely asserted that powers of this kind are generally limited by reference to the principle of propor-tionality: any interference with private rights should be strictly limited to what is demanded by the underlying general or public interest in that context. The Court of Justice has confirmed the applicability of this concept in the area of competition investigations.[20] In the *Orkem* case, Advocate General Darmon went so far as to say that 'the information requested by the Commission must *appear* to be connected with the infringement at issue'.[21] In those proceedings the Commission itself said that it did not undertake investigations as a means of 'probing'.[22]

Requests for information in practice need to be made in writing, to be copied to the authorities of the Member State where the party in question is resident or has its registered office (Article 11(2) of Regulation 17); the request will usually specify a time-limit for the supply of the information; and it must, under Article 11, state the legal basis and purpose of the request and give notice of the penalties for supplying any incorrect information. There is no duty to respond to such a request but failure to do so is likely to provoke a formal decision under Article 11(5), *requiring* the information. A decision under Article 11(5), like any other decision in the sense of Article 190 of the Treaty, has to be 'reasoned', and this may provide some scope for legal challenge, but it is probably sufficient to state in general terms the purpose for which the information is required.[23] In practice most requests for information have been complied with, but more recently the Commission has increasingly been forced to make use of its power under Article 11(5)[24] – thirty-one such decisions in 1987 for example, evidencing an escalating recalcitrance and resort to defensive legal argument based on procedural rights. Recent examples arise from the Commission's wide-ranging investigation into the thermoplastics industry,[25] when for instance the French company Orkem (formerly Chimie) refused to supply the bulk of the information requested in August 1987,[26] requiring a Commission decision under Article 11(5) the following November. There was a similar difficulty in gaining information from the Belgian company Solvay.[27]

The information sought under Article 11 may include documentary evidence.[28] Moreover, further information may be requested after an investigation under Article 14 has been carried out. While requests for information are likely to precede investigations, there is no reason why they should not be made subsequently.[29] Although the party concerned cannot be required to supply information not in its possession, it may on the other hand, in the view of Advocate General Darmon,[30] be required to organise such information as it does have for the benefit of the Commission's officials.

Investigations or inspections

If requests for information under Article 11 have not produced all the evidence necessary for the Commission's enquiry, it may resort to its powers of 'investigation' or 'inspection' under Article 14 of Regulation 17. Again, there are two levels of authorisation for the exercise of such powers: a written authorisation or 'simple mandate' under Article 14(2); and a formal decision from the Commission under Article 14(3), which is binding on the undertaking to whom it is addressed (Member State authorities may not be subject to inspection, only to requests for information). This is not, however, a two-stage procedure, in the sense that the Commission may proceed straightaway to a decision under Article 14(3). Such inspections in fact comprise powers of search, interrogation and verification. Article 14(1) enumerates the following specific powers – examination of books and business records; the taking of copies of or extracts from these materials; on the spot oral questions; and entry to land, premises and means of transport. The relevant Member State authorities have to be informed in good time before any such inspection is carried out and must know the identity of the Commission officials involved. National officials may be asked to assist in the inspection, under Article 14(5).

A written authorisation does not oblige the party under investigation to comply. This is implicit in Article 14 and is certainly the Commission's own view.[31] During the 1970s the majority of inspections were of this kind, by simple mandate, but since 1979 the Commission has made more use of its power of decision, moving towards a tougher policy of enforcement in relation to more covert behaviour.[32] Because of its compulsory nature the decision under Article 14(3) is likely to give rise to more legal argument. Given the possible consequences of a search, it is important for the undertakings in question to be informed of the subject-matter and purpose of the investigation, the date it will take place and the possible penalties and right to appeal. But, most significantly, the parties need not be informed in advance,[33] thus allowing 'surprise' investigations to take place. Nor does the Commission have to base its decision on detailed reasons, beyond what is stated as being the subject-matter and purpose of the investigation (for instance, the refusal to make certain books available during an inspection under Article 14(2) in the *AM & S Europe* case).[34] In the *National Panasonic* case Advocate General Warner was of the view that it was not incumbent on the Commission to actually state that it was acting under Article 14(3) because it feared that the company would otherwise destroy crucial evidence.[35]

Member State officials (such as officials from the Office of Fair Trading in the U.K.) are likely to be involved to some extent in these inspections. They must in any event be given prior notice and in the case of a decision taken under Article 14(3) be consulted beforehand (Article 14(4)). The Commission has stated that such consultation comprises: (a) notifying the national body of the planned investigation and the contents of the proposed decision; (b) giving the national authority the opportunity to submit its comments; and (c) taking note of such comments. The substance of the consultation is recorded in writing, as good administrative practice, but is not made available to any other parties. When the inspection takes place, assistance may be provided by the national authorities, at the request of either the latter or of the Commission;

this may be necessary in any case of recalcitrance on the part of an undertaking under investigation. Article 14(6) envisages a kind of enforcement which goes beyond the use of pecuniary sanctions: 'the Member State concerned shall afford the necessary assistance'. This will depend very much on what measures are available under the relevant national law and Article 14(6) also contemplates any necessary change in Member State law for this purpose (for instance, in the Netherlands, the legislation of 10 July 1968).[36] In the U.K. it has been assumed that the directly applicable nature of Regulation 17 renders any special measures unnecessary: an *ex parte* order compelling submission to the inspection would be available, and that in turn is backed up by contempt of court procedures. This is arguably a cumbersome process which may impede the effectiveness of surprise inspections, since it would require Commission inspectors to obtain *ex parte* orders in advance in such cases, in effect anticipating recalcitrance. The U.K. provision in this respect has therefore provoked some debate.[37]

The Commission's powers of investigation under Article 14 were subjected to close analysis in the arguments before the Court of Justice in the *Hoechst* case in 1989.[38] The companies involved in those proceedings, who had refused to allow the Commission officials access to certain information on three repeated occasions between January and April 1987, argued that there was a distinction between narrower powers of investigation and wider powers of search. This distinction (discussed further in Chapter 3) appears to be based upon the willingness of the party concerned to hand over information and any enforced production of information would correspond with the concept of a 'search' under some national laws.[39] However, the view of the Commission, accepted in essence by both Advocate General Mischo and the Court of Justice in the *Hoechst* case, was that the concept of investigation is a generic one which includes searches, the latter being simply a more far-reaching version of an investigation. Within the structure of Article 14 the crucial difference is to be found between paragraphs (2) and (3) on the one hand – which require information (voluntarily or under obligation) – and, on the other hand, paragraph (6), which may trigger the use of compulsion, if necessary, on the part of the Member State authorities to gain information. The Court identified three levels of investigation. Firstly, there is that of voluntary cooperation, and no problems arise in that respect. Secondly, there is the stage at which a decision under Article 14(3) proves necessary. In such a case:

the Commission's officials have, *inter alia*, the power to have shown to them the documents they request, to enter such premises as they choose, and to have shown to them the contents of any piece of furniture which they indicate. On the other hand, they may not obtain access to premises or furniture by force or oblige the staff of the undertaking to give them such access, or carry out searches without the permission of the management of the undertaking.[40]

Finally, if information or access has been refused, the Commission may invoke the aid of the relevant national authorities to use whatever powers they possess under Member State law to enforce the Commission's request.

In summary, then, Commission officials cannot roam around offices at will searching anywhere and everywhere. But they can say: 'Show us the documents relating to such-and-such a meeting', or 'Show us the contents of this filing cabinet', or 'Let us see those files we have just noticed through the window being loaded into that van outside'.[41] In the context of the investigation of sophisticated covert activity – increasingly a matter of concertation rather than open agreement – it is not the 'classic files' which are likely to provide crucial evidence, but 'loose pieces of paper' indicative of collusion: diaries, cryptic notes of meetings and the like. It is clear, therefore, that the Commission can ask for a great deal; but what its officials can forcibly extract will depend ultimately on the effectiveness and legal limitations of national procedures. The fact that it is the Commission's role to specify the information it wishes to see, and that there is a duty of cooperation under Article 14(3), means also that the party under investigation should take care not to destroy, hide or simply not mention information which it knows, or should know, is relevant to the Commission's purpose; such conduct could subsequently attract a fine for providing 'incomplete information'.

Notes

1 O.J. Special Edition 1959–62, p. 87.
2 See Chapter 9 in this volume.
3 Commission, *Fourteenth Report on Competition Policy* (1984), p. 51. For details, see Christopher Bellamy and Graham Child, *Common Market Law of Competition*, (3rd ed., 1987, Sweet & Maxwell), p. 22.
4 See Case 155/79, *AM & S Europe v Commission* (1982) E.C.R. 1575, for a discussion of the importance of this distinction.
5 See L. Neville Brown and J.F. Garner, *French Administrative Law* (3rd ed., 1983, Butterworths), Ch. 11.
6 See the discussion in Christopher Harding and Richard W. Ireland, *Punishment: Rhetoric, Rule and Practice* (1989, Routledge), pp. 158 – 159.
7 Commission Decision of 5 September 1980.
8 Case 48/69, *ICI v Commission* (1972) E.C.R. 619.
9 Cases 100–103/80, *Musique Diffusion Francaise v Commission* (1983) E.C.R. 1825.
10 Ibid., at p. 1920, and p. 1880, respectively. See also the remarks by Advocate General Vesterdorf in Case T-7/89, *Hercules Chemicals v Commission* (1992) 4 C.M.L.R. 84, that the Commission's internal allocation of its work could not be considered as violating any essential procedural rights (p. 103).
11 See, for example, Bellamy and Child, op. cit, Ch. 11.
12 Regulation 17/62, Article 15(5); Case 48/72, *Brasserie de Haecht v Wilkin (no. 2)* (1973) E.C.R. 77.
13 See Table 5.1 given in Chapter 5 of this volume.
14 (1976) 1 C.M.L.R. D95.

15 For instance, the British Transport and General Workers Union: see the Commission's *Sixteenth Report on Competition Policy* (1986), point 43.
16 See C.S. Kerse, *EEC Antitrust Procedure* (1st ed., 1981, European Law Centre), p. 55.
17 See, for example, Case 26/76, *Metro v Commission* (1977) E.C.R. 1875.
18 Ibid.; see also the discussion in Chapter 5 of this volume.
19 See Neville March Hunnings, 'The Stanley Adams Affair or the Biter Bit', 24 (1987) C.M.L.Rev. 65.
20 See, for example, Case 136/79, *National Panasonic v Commission* (1980) E.C.R. 2033; Case 155/79, *AM & S Europe v Commission* (1982); Case 374/87, *Orkem v Commission* (1989) E.C.R. 3283.
21 (1989) E.C.R., p. 3320.
22 Ibid., p. 332.
23 Case 31/59, *Brescia v High Authority*, (1960) E.C.R. 71.
24 Commission, *Seventeenth Report on Competition Policy* (1987), point 57.
25 O.J. 1989, L74/22.
26 See (1989) E.C.R., p. 3302.
27 Ibid.
28 Ibid., p. 3347.
29 Ibid.
30 Ibid., p. 3315.
31 O.J. 1979, C310/30 – 31 (Answer to Written Question 677/79).
32 See the remarks by Advocate General Warner, (1980) E.C.R. p. 2067.
33 Case 136/79, *National Panasonic v Commission* (1980).
34 (1982) E.C.R. 1575.
35 (1980) E.C.R., p. 2070.
36 Staatsblad 395.
37 P.J. Kuyper and T.P.J.N. van Rijn, 'Procedural Guarantees and Investigatory Methods, with special reference to Competition', 2 (1982) *Yearbook of European Law*, pp. 1 – 55; Advocate General Mischo in Cases 46/87 and 227/88, *Hoechst v Commission* (1989) E.C.R. 2859, p. 2892.
38 Cases 46/87 and 227/88, Hoechst v Commission (1989).
39 (1989) E.C.R., p. 2867.
40 Ibid., p. 2927.
41 Advocate General Mischo, ibid., p. 2879.

3 Investigations: legal control

The powers of investigation laid down for the Commission in relation to the enforcement of the Community's competition policy and other areas of action have been subjected to legal control principally through the scrutiny carried out by the European Court of Justice. During the last twenty years companies who have been subject to investigations have increasingly challenged the legality of different aspects of these procedures, thus giving the Court the opportunity – usually via the review process laid down in Articles 172 and 173 of the EEC Treaty – to apply general principles of legality and identify the content of the rights of those subject to such proceedings. The Court's case-law in this respect has drawn heavily on the comparable legal protection under the law of Member States and, where relevant, has made reference to the legal guarantees provided for in the European Convention on Human Rights and occasionally other international instruments. This is consistent with the Court's established approach to the question of the legal protection of individuals: that the standard of protection afforded to Community subjects should match that of the constitutional law of Member States, although worked out more precisely in a way which is relevant to the Community rather than any national context. In the words of Advocate General Vesterdorf, the task is to seek to ensure:

> ... within the framework formed by the existing body of rules and the judgements handed down hitherto ... that legal protection within the Community meets the standard otherwise regarded as reasonable in Europe.[1]

Underlying these developments, therefore, is an extensive exercise in comparative research coupled with an attempt to synthesize these findings into a suitable Community solution.

It is in this discussion of the kind of protection afforded at the national level that the problem of the juridical character of the Community procedures and powers is squarely confronted. Clearly, there are analogous powers of investigation exercised by various public authorities at the national level, but frequently this is in the context of a system of criminal law and criminal procedure. In some Member States, some such powers are formally described as being part of an administrative investigation rather than as a component of criminal law enforcement. While the 'administrative' model may, for the reasons mentioned in Chapter 1, appear as the most appropriate analogy for Community purposes, the distinction between criminal and administrative investigations is not sufficiently widespread among the Member States to justify a jettisoning of the 'criminal' model in the Community context. Indeed, to completely disregard the analogy of criminal proceedings would have important, and perhaps undesirable, consequences in relation to the issue of legal protection for those subject to such procedures. Without anticipating the detail of the following discussion, it may suffice to say for the present that the Court of Justice's approach has been relatively open-minded, so as to consider the whole range of analogous rules under national systems and not to give complete precedence to the solutions worked out at the national level in relation to 'administrative' or 'non-criminal law procedures'.

Another distinction sometimes drawn in arguments concerning legal protection, that between the rights of natural and corporate (or 'legal') persons, has also not been taken up by the Court of Justice. For instance, it is contested under both Belgian and Irish constitutional law whether the general principle of the inviolability of the home applies to legal persons and to business premises.[2] For the Court of Justice to follow that approach would have significant consequences in the Community context since the majority of those concerned in Community investigations are in the nature of things companies and not natural persons. The distinction also reflects difficult questions in the theory of legal protection, as to the lesser entitlement of corporate persons under some systems and as to the responsibility which may be imputed (whether for purposes of criminal or other liability) to corporate actors. A successful and coherent system of legal protection needs to work through these questions in making choices about the extent of legal protection.

The scheme of discussion which follows in this chapter will examine the kind of legal protection which has been provided to date in the jurisprudence of the European Court of Justice, by reference to different aspects of the investigation. It is possible to analyse these developments from the point of view of both the investigating authority (the Commission in this context) and the subject of the investigation. Both may be regarded as having rights in relation to the same issue and the essential legal problem is usually one of balancing these competing rights – the familiar scenario of constitutional protection. The basic rights in relation to investigations, as developed so far, may be listed in the following manner.

COMMISSION

1. The right to request information/to cooperation from those subject to the investigation

exceptions
- evidence which is self-incriminating;
- confidential ('privileged') information.

2. The right of entry into premises:

- the right of surprise;
- the right of forcible entry (as allowed under Member State law);
- the right of search.

SUBJECT OF INVESTIGATION

1. The right to refuse to provide certain information:

- self-incriminating evidence;
- confidential information.

2 The right to refuse entry (inviolability of private premises):

- the right to resist forcible entry without judicial authorisation;
- the right to seek review of the extent and manner of the investigation or search.

It can be seen that this analysis of the respective rights of the parties is based upon two major stages of investigation, namely requests for information and inspection of premises. Requests for information broadly speaking raise questions as to what kind of evidence may or may not be required by the Commission and the significant issues so far have been self-incrimination and confidentiality. On the other hand, inspections and entry to premises have given rise to questions concerned with the manner in which the investigation is carried out (although questions concerned with categories of obtainable evidence may also arise at this stage): typically, whether the inspection may be unannounced (the right of surprise, or conversely of prior warning); whether it may be carried out forcibly (the issue of judicial warrant); and the extent of the inspection (whether the investigation turns into a 'search'). It should be borne in mind that this scheme of analysis is deceptively neat: these issues have arisen in case-law at different times and the Court of Justice itself has not attempted to impose this kind of order in its own analysis of these questions.

The right to information and to cooperation during investigations

This is implied for the Commission in Articles 11 and 14 of Regulation 17, for instance in Article 11(4), where it is stated that the owners of undertakings, or their representatives, legal or otherwise, 'shall supply the information requested', and in Article 14(3), which provides that 'undertakings ... shall submit to investigations'. In legislative terms this follows from the imperative of ensuring a proper application of the Community's policies. Thus the

Commission 'may obtain all necessary information' (Article 11(1)) and 'may undertake all necessary investigations' (Article 14(1)). Generally, therefore, the Commission's right to information and cooperation is limited to what is necessary. This has been recognised on a number of occasions by the Court of Justice when it has affirmed that the principle of proportionality is applicable to Commission investigations.[3] However, it is also accepted that it is for the Commission to appraise the necessity for an investigation or certain aspects of it, subject to review by the Court as to whether measures actually adopted by the Commission have been excessive.[4] It remains unclear in practice how far the Court would be prepared to intervene to control the Commission's discretion in this respect. In his opinion in the *Orkem* case Advocate General Darmon pointed to two elements in the Court's review of this discretion: first, that the subject-matter of the request for information must appear to be connected with the infringement at issue; and second, that the extent of the information required is not manifestly excessive for purposes of the investigation.[5] The main purpose here seems to be to guard against incidental searches and 'fishing expeditions'.

In the *Orkem* proceedings it was argued that the Commission's investigation had gone further than was necessary, especially in view of the fact that the Commission had already indicated to the parties under investigation that it had evidence that they had engaged in a concerted practice. But the Court affirmed that the Commission in such a case retained the discretion to decide on the necessity for certain evidence:

> Even if it already has evidence, or indeed proof, of the existence of an infringement, the Commission may legitimately take the view that it is necessary to request further information to enable it better to define the scope of the infringement, to determine its duration or to identify the circle of undertakings involved.[6]

This argument was amplified in the opinion of Advocate General Darmon, who emphasised that the Court can only review the need for evidence in relative terms. Moreover, he went on to argue that it was not merely a question of establishing the basic fact of an infringement: it was also necessary to verify its extent, the number of persons involved and its duration, especially for purposes of determining the application and gravity of any penalties. This followed, in his view, from two duties which were incumbent upon the Commission: the first, to carry out a specifically 'repressive' role (that is, to prosecute individual cases in which an infringement had taken place); the second, to fulfil the wider task of ensuring that the competition rules were applied .[7] Viewed in this way the necessity for the investigation may be more generously interpreted.

It seems that the line which must be drawn in terms of necessity and proportionality is between investigation based upon evidence (or, it may be termed, 'reasonable grounds for suspicion') and investigation which is simply 'probing' or 'fishing' for evidence. It is not acceptable for the Commission to say to itself: 'We are generally suspicious of the behaviour of this company; we have no hard evidence, however; but let us look around its offices to see what we can dig up'. Since the Commission's authorisation or decision must, in the wording of Articles 11 and 14, 'specify' the subject-matter and purpose of the inquiry or inspection, it would appear difficult on that ground alone to justify a random casting around for evidence, or 'fishing expedition'. Arguments based on proportionality and necessity would, it is suggested, categorically exclude such a power.[8]

Apart from the general need to ensure the necessity and proportionality of requests for information and cooperation, the Commission's right to obtain information is further limited by reference to specific categories of evidence which may be legitimately withheld. To date, two main exceptions of this kind have been established in favour of parties subject to these proceedings: information which is self-incriminating, and that which is confidential or 'privileged'. These exceptions are better understood in terms of the *individual*'s rights to guard against self-incrimination and to protection of confidential information.

Self-incrimination

The right to refuse to incriminate oneself in the context of investigations into alleged offences is widely stated in national legal systems, albeit to a varying extent. It is a well-developed constitutional right in American law, for instance (although, interestingly, not available there to corporate bodies, as it is under German law),[9] but often to a lesser extent under the law of Community Member States. The corollary of the right not to incriminate oneself is the obligation to assist in a public investigation, a duty which arises in the present context under Articles 11(5) and 14(3) of Regulation 17. It would be logical to start from the premiss that there is such a general duty, as a good citizen to assist such inquiries and to provide certain kinds of information, but to admit that this obligation may be qualified in order to ensure fair treatment of individuals.

The issue was raised squarely before the Court of Justice in the *Orkem* and *Solvay* cases in 1989.[10] Both of these defendant companies, investigated by the Commission as part of its probe into the thermoplastics industry, maintained that there existed under Community law a right to silence or not give evidence against oneself, even though not explicitly provided for in any Community legislation. This was in effect an invitation to the Court to discover such a principle of legal protection in the general fund of basic Community principles, and so necessarily required a major jurisprudential enquiry on the part of the Court.

There was little doubt that in itself Community legislation, or more specifically Regulation 17, did not provide for such a right to stay silent. This legislative position had been consciously adopted by the Council in the face of a resolution by the European Parliament that:

any person required to supply the information may refuse to answer the questions where the reply is liable to expose them ... to criminal penalties.[11]

This resolution was based on the recommendation of the Parliament's Internal Market Committee (the 'Deringer Report'),[12] which argued that otherwise the Regulation would be declared void by the Court of Justice. However, the Council was unswayed by this view; in the subsequent argument of Advocate General Warner, to have admitted such a right would have rendered the Commission's powers largely ineffective.[13] The Court's task in 1989, therefore, was to determine whether there was after all a superior general principle of Community law which would justify and require such a limitation of the Commission's powers.

In order to rule upon the existence of such a principle, the Court was referred to a number of sources: the position generally within the legal systems of the Member States, and any relevant international legal instruments, in this case the International Covenant on Civil and Political Rights and the European Convention on Human Rights. It should be borne in mind here that any Community principle should not be based directly on such sources, but that they should be used to achieve a result which is appropriate to the Community context.[14]

Advocate General Darmon's analysis is full and useful, but shows that any conclusions to be drawn from a comparative survey are far from categorical. The important questions to be asked are: (1) is there generally a right of silence under the laws of the Member States? (2) if so, does it extend to corporate persons? (3) does it extend to 'administrative' as well as criminal proceedings? and (4) does it extend to the stage of 'administrative investigation' as well as that of 'determination'? It was clear from the Advocate General's survey that the overall legal position is variable throughout the Member States, but whether this is so to the extent of appearing as a 'mosaic of national approaches' may be questioned.[15] The main problem is surely that some systems make use of administrative procedures and sanctions (as does the Community) to deal with competition infringements and do not allow the right to silence in relation to such administrative procedures. The essential question is therefore whether the use of non-criminal proceedings in itself justifies a lower level of legal protection for the parties subject to such proceedings, and this is also the hub of the argument when any attempt is made to apply the provisions of the International Covenant and the European Convention. Advocate General Darmon felt able to exclude any resort to Article 14(3) of the International Covenant on the ground that the Covenant does not apply to corporate persons, and also doubted whether that provision was intended to apply to administrative proceedings in competition matters (a less convincing argument, especially if the Covenant is given a progressive interpretation). Reference to Article 6 of the European Convention raises the same issue: would paragraphs (2) and (3) of that provision apply to non-criminal proceedings? The Advocate General was not prepared to be persuaded by the reasoning of the European Court of Human Rights in its *Ozturk* judgement in 1984 on this issue,[16] stating that the latter had given a 'rather wide definition of the concept of a person 'accused of a criminal offence".[17] It will be necessary to return later to this fundamental distinction between criminal and administrative proceedings; it is sufficient to note here that Advocate General Darmon favoured a narrow definition of 'criminal proceeding' so as to exclude a reliance on international treaty provisions which might justify the importation of a right to silence.

The judgement of the Court of Justice in *Orkem* took the same view as the Advocate General as regards what could be derived from Member State law or international treaties, but decisively took the argument a stage further by considering the general rights of defence of parties in such proceedings. The thrust of the Court's reasoning was that the rights of defence at the contentious stage of these proceedings must not be irremediably undermined during the investigation procedure. As a consequence, the Court appears to be saying that there is a right to silence, at least in relation to questions which in effect seek admission from the parties concerned that they have engaged in a prohibited anti-competitive practice. That is for the Commission to prove by means of evidence other than the parties' own statements. To illustrate the point, reference may be made to the 'incriminating' questions posed to Orkem and Solvay, which the Court considered to undermine their rights of defence. For instance, Question 1(c) in Section 11 of the Commission's decision sought clarification of 'every step or concerted measure ... adopted to support such price initiatives'; any answer would have been an acknowledge-ment of involvement in a price-fixing arrangement. Similarly Questions 1 and 2 of Section 111 asked for details of 'any system or method used to achieve targets or quotas as between the parties' and any answer would have been tantamount to an admission of market sharing.[18]

The *Orkem* and *Solvay* judgements therefore confirm that there is a right to avoid self-incrimination and that this right is integral to the fairness of Community competition proceedings rather than being simply derivative of Member State and other law. The Court of Justice has taken the initiative in pushing Community law ahead of some other systems in this respect, and has tacitly acknowledged the significance of the proceedings in question, so as to justify this guarantee to the defence.

The right of confidential communication: 'legal professional privilege'

In the context of Commission investigations, the issue of confidentiality has arisen in relation to information which is confidential as between lawyers and their clients and as such is protected under a number of national legal systems under the heading of 'legal professional privilege' (*secret professionel*). Confidentiality between lawyer and client is recognised in principle under the law of all the Member States on the basis that any protection of individual rights requires a full and uninhibited consultation between individuals and their lawyers, so as to ensure the independence of legal advice. It is open to argument whether this right of confidentiality may be termed 'fundamental': following his survey of relevant Member State law and doctrine,[19] Advocate General Warner categorised it as 'a right not lightly to be denied, but not one so entrenched that, in the Community, the Council could never legislate to override or modify it.' Certainly it is not listed in any of the Member State constitutions or in the European Convention on Human Rights.

The legal practice of the Member States, or at least that of the first nine states summarised in the *AM & S Europe* case before the Court of Justice in 1982,[20] allows generally for confidentiality of communications between lawyer and client, but its extent and the circumstances in which it may be claimed vary from one system to another or within a particular system. Just to illustrate this point briefly: under English law, the client may waive the right to confidentiality; under French law, such waiver by itself is not decisive, since the lawyer retains a discretion whether or not to disclose the contents of the communication. Within the U.K., some statutory powers of investigation are subject to the right of confidential communication without any qualification (for instance, under s. 85 of the Fair Trading Act 1973 and ss 3 and 7 of the Competition Act 1980); whereas under the Finance Act, in relation to investigation for tax purposes, the right is subject to some modification. It was never to be seriously doubted, therefore, that once the subject had been raised, as it was eventually in 1982, that some kind of principle of confidential communication would need to be stated for Community law. The main question would concern its extent. A great deal of argument was produced for the *AM & S Europe* case, with the British Government and the Consultative Committee of the Bars and Law Societies of the European Community (the CCBE) intervening on behalf of the applicant, and the French Government intervening on behalf of the Commission.

The Court of Justice readily accepted a basic principle of confidential communication. It qualified the application of the principle in the Community context by saying that it was available in respect of: (1) confidential communications between a lawyer and client; (2) made for the purposes and in the interests of the latter's right of defence; and (3) by independent lawyers (that is, not lawyers employed by the 'client').[21] To be privileged, then, communications must relate to a proceeding initiated by the Commission, or at least to the possibility of such a proceeding. The Court applied this test favourably to AM & S Europe's correspondence, which was:

> principally concerned with how far it might be possible to avoid conflict between the applicant and the Community authorities on the applicant's position, in particular with regard to the Community provisions on competition. In spite of the time which elapsed between the said communications and the initiation of a procedure, those circumstances are sufficient to justify considering the communications as falling within the context of the rights of defence and the lawyers' specific duties in that connection.[22]

Moreover, the lawyer in question was not an in-house lawyer employed by the company and so satisfied the criterion of independent legal advice laid down by the Court. In-house communications may clearly be used as evidence by the Commission. In the case of *Deere & Co.*,[23] the defendant company's knowledge of the illegality of its conduct was evidenced by its advice from its in-house lawyer that its export ban was contrary to EEC rules.

However, the recognition of the right of confidential communication in the above terms does not resolve all of the issues connected with the exercise of that right, since there remains the important practical problem of how the confidential nature of the documents is attested during the investigation. Should the Commission simply accept the other party's word for the privileged character of the contents of a particular document? The Commission itself, both the Advocate Generals who presented opinions in the *AM & S Europe* case (Warner and Slynn), and the Court were all clear that the issue could not depend in this way on the *ipse dixit* of the party under investigation. On the other hand, the Advocate Generals regarded it as unrealistic to argue that the Commission's inspectors could look at the disputed documents, decide that they were in fact privileged and then put them out of mind; nor was it sufficiently persuasive that the inspector would be from a Commission directorate other than that which would decide upon the infringement (which was the case in 1982). Both opinions insisted that the matter, if disputed, should be referred to an impartial tribunal, although it was Advocate General Slynn's recommendation that it be the Court of Justice itself, rather than that of Advocate General Warner that it be a national court, which was adopted by the Court in its judgement.

The position in practice was described by Advocate General Slynn:

> In the majority of cases the parties are likely to be able to reach agreement as to whether a document is in fact within the principle, the undertaking's lawyer being able to satisfy the inspector as to the nature of the document, without disclosing the contents. If disputes arise, the Commission, if not satisfied, can take a decision which can be referred to the Court, as was done in this case ....[24]

Although this approach neatly places the issue in the hands of the Court of Justice, it may however be asked what kind of jurisdiction the Court is then exercising. The decision comes before the Court under Article 173 of the EEC Treaty, under which the Court is to rule on its legality. Yet in effect the Court is deciding a question of fact: whether or not the document is privileged. The Commission had already objected to this possibility, arguing that it was the well-settled case-law of the Court itself that it was the role of the Commission to be the tribunal of first instance in all competition questions.[25] Despite this argument the Court without any comment awarded itself in the *AM & S Europe* judgement the jurisdiction to examine the documents and decide their status – in effect developing its own jurisdiction by allowing for a role of verification as well as legal assessment under Article 173. Arguably, this was the only way out of the dilemma. To allow the Commission to determine the issue would not have enabled justice to be seen to be done; to refer it to national courts would not have ensured a uniformity of approach and may have resulted in delays if it was then necessary to resort to the Article 177 reference procedure.[26]

One further aspect of the principle which emerged from the *AM & S Europe* case may be briefly considered here. The Court's statement of the principle is limited to communications with lawyers 'entitled to practise in one of the Member States'.[27] Problems therefore arise in relation to communications with lawyers in non-EEC countries, and this is not likely to be a minor issue in view of the number of North American and Japanese undertakings who tangle with the EEC competition rules. Recognising this problem, the Commission therefore asked the Council to authorise it to negotiate agreements between the EEC and third countries in relation to the protection of legal papers in connection with the application of the competition rules.[28]

The right of entry into premises

It has already been noted that the Commission has increasingly had to resort to powers under Article 14 of Regulation 17 to obtain information not voluntarily supplied to it upon request by entering and if necessary searching private premises. Inevitably such measures have provoked a number of legal arguments concerning the exercise of these powers and the extent to which such intrusion is justified in the light of the basic principle of the inviolability of private premises guaranteed under Member State legal systems. A number of specific issues have arisen, notably the legality of raids without warning, of searches within premises, and the use of forcible entry. But it would be useful in the first instance to discuss the applicability of the general principle of inviolability of private premises.

Since this principle would appear to underlie the more specific arguments, it is perhaps surprising that it has been raised in argument before the Court of Justice only at a relatively late date in the *Hoechst* case in 1989, arising out of the Commission's investigation into the PVC and Polyethylene Cartel. The German company Hoechst, a member of this major cartel, had refused to allow Commission officials to enter its Frankfurt offices for a period of over two months in early 1987 and later attempted to justify this recalcitrance by appealing to its fundamental right to the inviolability of its business premises. The company argued that this basic right was common to the legal systems of the Member States, should be applied to business premises as much as to homes, and ought to be incorporated into the Community system of legal protection. The Commission agreed with this proposition;[29] the only argument concerned the limits which could be placed on the exercise of this right, and in particular the need for a court order to enter such premises (which is discussed further below).

For present purposes it may simply be noted that the general principle may be derived from the following national provisions: Article 10 of the Belgian Constitution; Article 72 of the Danish Constitution; Article 13 of the German Constitution; Article 9(1) of the Greek Constitution of 1975; Article 18(2) of the Spanish Constitution of 1978; Article 66 of the French Constitution (implied); Article 40(5) of the Irish Constitution; Article 14 of the Italian Constitution; Article 15 of the Luxembourg Constitution; Article 12 of the Dutch Constitution; Article 34(2) of the Portuguese Constitution of 1976; and from Article 8 of the European Convention on Human Rights. It should also be noted, however, that there is some doubt as to whether the business premises of legal persons are covered by this protection, or at least its stricter forms, under some of these constitutional provisions (in the case of Belgium, Greece, Luxembourg and Portugal), while interpretation of the relevant provisions in Ireland and the Netherlands clearly excludes the protection of business premises. The issue has yet to be tested under the European Convention. This element of doubt, though, is probably academic for purposes of Community law. As Advocate General Mischo noted in *Hoechst*:

> a general trend is discernible in the national legal systems towards the assimilation of business premises to a home. In any event, in the great majority of Member States, the inspection of business premises is made subject, by virtue of special legislation, to more or less stringent formal or procedural conditions.[30]

He therefore agreed with the Commission that it should be expressly accepted that at the Community level there is a fundamental right to the inviolability of business premises. The Court was less categorical in its judgement, however, preferring to see Article 8 of the European Convention as being concerned with a man's 'personal freedom', but it did go on to confirm that there was a basic protection against arbitrary or disproportionate intervention in the case of business premises. In practical terms there would seem to be no difference between the Court's position and that adopted by Advocate General Mischo and the Commission. Corporate premises are entitled in principle to inviolability. But, as is usually the case in situations of constitutional protection, it is in the working out of the exceptions to this guarantee, in a more general interest, that the problems reside.

The issue of prior warning: the Commission's right of surprise

The wording of Article 14 does not require the Commission to give prior warning to an undertaking that it proposes to carry out an inspection of its premises, but the relevant Member State authorities must be advised beforehand and in practice a national official will usually accompany the Commission's inspectors. On arrival the latter must present the undertaking's representatives with the Commission's decision ordering the investigation and this must specify the subject-matter and purpose of the inspection. However, it need not go so far as to state that the inspection was without notice since the Commission feared that otherwise the evidence might be hidden or destroyed.[31] On the face of it, therefore, Article 14 entitles the Commission to carry out surprise inspections, 'dawn raids' or whatever term is used to describe investigations on an undertaking's premises without prior notice.

Since the end of the 1970s the Commission has resorted increasingly to this tactic, a reaction to a higher level of covert behaviour on the part of companies.[32] The legality of surprise raids was challenged in 1979 by National Panasonic, a British subsidiary of the Japanese electrical manufacturer Matsushita. Commission officials, accompanied by an officer from the Office of Fair Trading, arrived unexpectedly at National Panasonic's office in Slough at ten o'clock one morning and proceeded to carry out the inspection without waiting for the arrival of the company's lawyer. This visitation gave rise to the legal challenge before the Court of Justice in which the company asserted that its basic rights had been infringed by the surprise nature of the Commission's visit. An attempt was made by National Panasonic to relate the claimed right to prior warning to the guarantee under Article 8 of the European Convention on Human Rights of respect for private and family life, home and correspondence. Advocate General Warner accepted that such a right, in so far as it could be translated into Community law, also extended to business premises;[33] the Court itself had already accepted that much by implication in an earlier judgement relating to investigations in the context of the Coal and Steel Community.[34] But at the same time the qualification of that guarantee, contained in Article 8(2) of the Convention, in the interest, *inter alia*, of the 'economic well-being of the country' had also to be imported into the Community context, and it is such an interest which can be used to justify the intrusion, even unannounced, by officials carrying out powers of inspection. Otherwise, in the words of the Advocate General:

> most of the powers of inspection and search conferred on national authorities, such as police, fiscal, public health and weights and measures authorities, quite apart from those concerned with the enforcement of competition law, would be invalid.[35]

In its judgement the Court was clearly of the view that the general interest of effective enforcement of the EEC competition rules justifed the Commission's power to carry out an inspection without notification.

The Commission's 'right of surprise' reasonably encompasses its ability to gain access to documentary evidence which it suspects may otherwise be withheld from an investigation. Whether it may extend to the possibility of surprising people into oral divulgences by means of on-the-spot questions is another matter. Article 14 allows the Commission to ask for 'oral explanations on the spot', which may of course lead company personnel to provide ill-considered answers, especially if they do not have the benefit of legal advice at that moment. The Commission's 'explanatory note' to Article 14(3) inspections supplies the Commission's view on the role of legal advisers:

> Any delay pending a lawyer's arrival must be kept to the strict minimum, and shall be allowed only where the management of the undertaking simultaneously undertakes to ensure that the business records will remain in the place and state they were in when the Commission officials arrived .... If the undertaking has an in-house legal service, Commission officials are instructed not to delay the investigation by awaiting the arrival of an external legal adviser.[36]

This is an attempt to balance the Commission's power to carry out an inspection without warning with the general right to legal representation. Clearly the Commission does not wish the necessity for some kind of legal presence to be used as an evasive tactic. Yet it could be argued that adequate rights of defence require that individuals should be given some time to consider answers to on-the-spot questions. The very nature of a surprise inspection would not allow the questions to be given in advance; the safeguards in this respect must lie in the allowance for a reasonable level of legal representation and recognition of the right not to incriminate oneself, discussed above.

The Commission's 'warrant' and the question of forcible entry

It is the Commission itself which authorises the investigation; it does not have to be approved by the warrant of an independent judicial authority. This would be a requirement under the criminal procedure of a number of the Member States (it is stated for instance under the German Constitution) and it had been argued in the 'Deringer Report' on the drafting of Regulation 17[37] that such a requirement ought to be imported into Community procedures involving the investigation of private premises, and Advocate General Warner in the *National Panasonic* case was surprised at the absence of a system of judicial warrant.[38] But this was not the view eventually taken by the Council when the Regulation was adopted and the necessity for the investigation and its allowable scope, if they are to be judged at all, have to be assessed *ex post facto* by the Court of Justice.

The question then arises as to whether such control after the event is sufficiently effective. The alternative approach – a system of judicial warrants – would require the Commission to make out a convincing case beforehand for its search before a judicial body. The arguments in favour of this approach are firstly one of constitutional necessity (a *per se* requirement) and secondly that based upon an empirically demonstrated practical necessity. The latter would not be easy to show, since in cases of review in the past, the Court of Justice has not found that the Commission has acted in violation of the principles of proportionality and necessity, and the Commission itself seems to behave with circumspection in the knowledge that its decision is open to review. The argument that a judicial warrant should be a *per se* requirement is also difficult to sustain. Many of the Member State laws, while requiring a judicial warrant for entry into a private dwelling, do not as regards the inspection of business premises in relation to such matters as competition and revenue (for instance, Belgium, Greece, Ireland, Luxembourg, the Netherlands and Spain). In a few states, a warrant is required to enter business premises if force is used (the U.K.) or if the investigation is classified as a 'search' (France and Italy – the concept of 'search' is discussed further below). The German Law on Restrictions of Competition (GWB) of 1957 also draws the distinction between an investigation and a search, but even where a warrant is required in principle exceptions are permitted. Article 46(4) of the Law provides that:

> Searches may be made only by order of the judge of the Local Court .... If danger of delay exists [officials of the Cartel Authority] may conduct the necessary searches during business hours without judicial order.

And Article 55 allows the Cartel Authority to seize material which could be of significance as evidence, and judicial confirmation should be sought subsequently if the person affected has explicitly objected to the seizure. Overall, therefore, there would seem to be little support under Member State law for the necessity of a judicial warrant in the context of competition investigations *as a matter of principle*, contrary to the urgings of the Deringer Committee when Regulation 17 was first being drafted.

The requirement for a judicial warrant was argued squarely before the Court of Justice in the *Dow Chemica Iberica* case in 1989.[39] Here it was urged that the Community principle of proportionality should be understood with reference to the requirement contained in Article 18(2) of the Spanish Constitution that investigations and searches could be opposed unless the party concerned had been caught in the act of committing an infringement or a court order had been issued in advance. It was suggested that an order could be obtained either from the Court of Justice or from a national court; in either case the Commission could be required to submit to certain minimal procedural guarantees. Both the Court and Advocate General Mischo dealt with this argument simply by stating that the content of the Community principle of proportionality could not be dictated by the requirements of one national system alone.[40] A related argument in this proceeding was based on an allegation of unfair treatment, on the assumption that the Commission was required to obtain a judicial warrant in some Member States but not in others. It was said, for instance, that such a court order was necessary in Denmark. The Commission, in its pleading, denied that this was a requirement of Danish law.[41] While the Court did not feel that it was necessary to consider that point directly, the Advocate General pointed out that *if there was* such a difference of treatment as between Member States, this was not an unlawful discrimination resulting from Community action, but simply a reflection of procedural differences at a national level.[42]

These arguments may be summarised by saying that as a matter of Community law no judicial warrant is required for the Commission's investigation of private premises; it is a matter for the Commission's own appraisal, subject to possible later review by the Court of Justice. However, in so far as Member State authorities are involved in the investigation, they may be subject to conditions of local law; but this is only likely to present a problem if a company is refusing any access, in which case the Commission can only proceed to carry out the inspection forcibly under the conditions laid down in national law. Thus in the case of the notoriously recalcitrant Hoechst company in 1989 it was necessary for the Bundeskartellamt to apply for a judicial order from the Amtsgericht of Frankfurt to allow itself and the Commission to forcibly carry out the inspection on the company's premises. The Court of Justice stated clearly in its *Hoechst* judgement that:

> if the Commission intends, with the assistance of the national authorities, to carry out an investigation other than with the cooperation of the undertakings concerned, it is required to respect the relevant procedural guarantees laid down by national law.[43]

And 'relevant procedural guarantees' may well include the requirement for a judicial warrant before a forcible search may be carried out. It should be emphasised that at such a stage in the procedure there is therefore a collaboration between legal systems, with a significant input of national law. Any differences between Member State law in this respect may be a matter of concern, although Advocate General Mischo in *Dow Chemical Iberica* did not consider that they would amount to an unlawful discrimination under Article 7 of the EEC Treaty. But while on the one hand it is true, as the Advocate General argued, that undertakings themselves, in choosing to be recalcitrant, contribute to the resulting inequality of treatment, it remains the case that different levels of procedural guarantee under national law may place some undertakings under a relative legal disadvantage. It is an inescapable fact that, if under the law of state x the conditions for the issue of a judicial warrant are more rigorous than under that of state y, then undertakings in state x are in a legally stronger position than those in state y. And this could have consequences for the *effectiveness* of the Commission's investigation. The Court of Justice hinted at this problem in its *Hoechst* judgement: ' ... Member States are required to ensure that the Commission's action is effective.'[44] If the Commission itself has any doubts on that score, presumably it should raise the issue with the member state concerned (as was proposed, apparently, in relation to intended legislation on *ex parte* orders in the U.K.).[45]

There is a further practical consideration if it is necessary to obtain a judicial warrant under national law in order to gain entry to premises. The point was made succintly by Advocate General Mischo in *Hoechst*:

Since Hoechst has set an example, there is a danger that, in the future, the machinery of Article 14(3) will be rendered inoperative in practice by the proliferation of formal objections on the part of undertakings. They are likely to require on each occasion the production of a search warrant, with the result that the Commission will lose the advantage of surprise. The risk is that the investigations will thus prove fruitless.[46]

The most straightforward way in which to guard against this problem is for the Commission to seek a court order in advance if it considers that there may be any objection.[47] But it has also been argued that it would be more logical for the Court of Justice to issue a 'European search warrant', since the Court is in any case the body which has the power to review the decision by the Commission ordering an investigation.[48] It is argued at the same time that there already exists the precedent for such a procedure under Article 81 of the European Atomic Energy Community Treaty, in relation to safety inspections.

> If the carrying out of an inspection is opposed, the Commission shall apply to the President of the Court of Justice for an order to ensure that the inspection be carried out compulsorily. The President of the Court of Justice shall give a decision within three days.
> If there is a danger in delay, the Commission may itself issue a written order, in the form of a decision, to proceed with the inspection. This order shall be submitted without delay to the President of the Court of Justice for subsequent approval.

However, authority for a 'European search warrant' would have to come from the Council, for instance in an amendment of Regulation 17 to make provision for such a power. It is open to question how willing the Council would be to agree to this development. It would, after all, represent a curtailment of the existing power of the Member State judiciary in a sensitive area of law enforcement. Theoretically at least, such a solution does have the attraction of overcoming the potential problem of lack of uniformity in Member State law relating to search warrants.

The concept of a 'search'

As noted in the previous chapter, in a number of the arguments before the Court of Justice concerning the Commission's powers of investigation, a distinction has been drawn between an 'investigation' and a 'search', the latter being understood as a much more intrusive exercise of powers which should therefore be subject to greater legal control. The distinction is drawn in the law of some of the Member States. For instance, Article 46 of the German statute on restrictions of competition refers to a power of investigation (*Einsichts-und Prüfungsrecht*) as distinct from the power to carry out a search (*Durchsuchungsrecht*). The classic definition of the concept of search in

German law is to be found in a judgement of the Bundesverfassungsgericht in 1979,[49] according to which a search is

> carried out with a precise objective and purpose ... to find persons or objects or to ascertain facts, so as to discover something that the occupant of the dwelling in which the search takes place does not wish to disclose or hand over himself.

'Investigation', on the other hand, presupposes cooperation in the inspection. The French law of 1986[50] distinguishes between entry in order to demand access to documents and the making of copies (Article 47) and the seizure of materials (Article 48), and requires prior judicial authorisation for the latter. Italian law differentiates between 'verification' and 'inspection' (*accertamenti, ispezioni*) on the one hand, and 'search' (*perquisizione*), such as the power to open locked doors and files, on the other hand, and again the latter process requires a judicial warrant. The gist of the difference therefore seems to reside in the need to extract information from an unwilling party: 'If you will not show us such documents or answer these questions, we must examine the files or seek out specific items in your office for ourselves'.[51] A search may therefore be understood as an investigation of an unwilling or uncooperative subject, which may therefore involve forcible action and hence may well be subject to a requirement of judicial authorisation.

In terms of the procedure laid down in Regulation 17, the relevant provision is Article 14(6), which refers to an undertaking's lack of co-operation and the consequent need to invoke the aid of national authorities. The special concept of 'search', understood as forcible investigation, may give rise to the need for a judicial warrant, the legal implications of which were discussed in the preceding section. In its *Hoechst* judgement, the Court of Justice was in no doubt that the Commission's powers under Regulation 17 extended to what is referred to as a 'search' under the law of some Member States:

> ... right of access would serve no useful purpose if the Commission's officials could do no more than ask for documents or files which they could identify precisely in advance. On the contrary, such a right implies the power to search for various items of information which are not already known or fully identified. Without such a power, it would be impossible for the Commission to obtain the information necessary to carry out the investigation if the undertakings concerned refused to cooperate or adopted an obstructive attitude.[52]

It may well be, as Advocate General Mischo hinted, that the precedent set by Hoechst in 1987 will render such powers of 'search' more necessary in the future.

Legal representation

While the right to legal representation is crucial at the later stage of the formal hearing (and is guaranteed in that context by Article 9(2) of Regulation 99 of 1963), there is less certainty about the extent of such a right in the earlier stages of a competition proceeding. Article 6 of the Commission's *Explanatory Notes to Article 14(2) and (3)* acknowledges the right to consult a legal adviser, but it is not overriding; that is, it is not a precondition for the validity of the investigation and must not be used as a delaying tactic. In the *National Panasonic* case the Court confirmed implicitly, and Advocate General Warner stated explicitly that there was no fundamental right to prepare for an investigation by taking legal advice or to ensure that 'suitable senior executives and lawyers' can be present when an inspection takes place.[53] Bearing in mind that there is a duty to comply with investigations only if a decision has been taken under Article 14(3), it is only in the circumstances of an Article 14(3) decision that the absence of a lawyer may be a matter of serious concern. Otherwise, the party under investigation may simply refuse to comply with the inspection until a lawyer can be present.

Notes

1 Case T-7/89, *Re the Polypropylene Cartel, Hercules Chemicals v Commission* (1992) 4 C.M.L.R. 84, p. 101. This builds upon earlier case law, e.g., Case 11/70, *Internationale Handelsgesellschaft v EVSt*, (1970) E.C.R. 1125; Case 4/73, *Nold v Commission*, (1974) E.C.R. 491.

2 (1989) E.C.R., p. 2885, and p. 2889.

3 Cases 5–11, 13–15/62, *San Michele and others v High Authority* (1962) E.C.R. 449, 460; Case 136/79, *National Panasonic v Commission*, (1980) E.C.R. 2033.

4 Case 155/79, *AM & S Europe v Commission*, (1982) E.C.R. 1575, 1610; Cases 46/87 and 227/88, *Hoechst v Commission* (1989) E.C.R., p. 2924; and see the discussion by Advocate General Darmon in Cases 375/87 and 27/88, *Orkem, Solvay v Commission*, (1989) E.C.R., p. 3318 *et seq.*

5 (1989) E.C.R., p. 3320.

6 Ibid., p. 3348.

7 Ibid., at p. 3330.

8 For a restrictive interpretation of the Commission's powers in this context, see Thiesing, Schroter and Hochbaum, *Les ententes et les positions dominantes dans le droit de la CEE* (1977, Jupiter, ed. Navarre), pp. 494–95.

9 On the rule against self-incrimination under the Fifth Amendment to the U.S. Constitution, and its exceptions, see C. Herman Pritchett, *Constitutional Civil Liberties* (1984, Prentice-Hall), pp. 198–204.

10 See cases referred to in note 4, above.

11 J.O. 1961, 15.11.61, p. 1406.

12 Doc. No. 57, 7.9.61., Eur. Parl.

13 Case 155/79, (1982) E.C.R., p. 1621; see generally the discussion by Asteris Pliakos, *Les droits de la défense et le droit communautaire de la concurrence* (1987, Bruylant).

14 See cases referred to in note 1, above.

15 Advocate General Darmon, (1989) E.C.R. p. 3332.

16 *Ozturk v Germany* (1984), 6 *European Human Rights Reports* 409.
17 (1989) E.C.R., p. 3337. But the European Commission on Human Rights has not contradicted this approach: see Case 13258/87, *M & Co. v Germany*, 9 February 1990, where it stated that the E.C. Commission was not a tribunal in the sense of Article 6 of the Convention.
18 Ibid., p. 3350.
19 In Case 155/79, (1982) E.C.R., pp. 1630–37.
20 (1982) E.C.R. 1575.
21 But cf the view of Advocate General Slynn, (1982) E.C.R., p. 1655.
22 (1982) E.C.R., p. 1614.
23 1985 O.J., L35/58; (1985) 2 C.M.L.R. 554.
24 (1982) E.C.R., p. 1663.
25 Ibid., pp. 11594–95.
26 As regards confidentiality vis-à-vis intervenors in appeals to the Court of First Instance, see the Order of the Court of First Instance in Case T30/89, *Hilti v Commission* (1990) E.C.R. 11–163.
27 (1982) E.C.R. p. 1612.
28 COM (84) 548 final, 9.10.1984; Jonathan Faull, 'Legal Professional Privilege (AM & S): the Commission Proposes International Negotiations', 10 (1985) E.L.Rev. 119; Commission, *Thirteenth Report on Competition Policy* (1983), p. 64.
29 (1989) E.C.R., p. 2870.
30 Ibid., p. 2893.
31 Case 136/79, *per* Advocate General Warner, (1980) E.C.R, p. 2070.
32 See (1980) E.C.R. p. 2067.
33 Ibid., p. 2068.
34 Case 31/59, *Acciaierria Di Brescia v High Authority* (1960) E.C.R., 71, 80.
35 (1980) E.C.R., p. 2068.
36 *Thirteenth Report on Competition Policy* (1983), Annex.
37 Doc. No. 57, 7.9.61, Eur. Parl.
38 (1980) E.C.R., p. 2068.
39 Cases 97-99/87. *Dow Chemica Iberica* (1989) E.C.R. 3165.
40 (1989) E.C.R., 3191, 2912.
41 Ibid., p. 3179.
42 Ibid., p. 2913.
43 (1989) E.C.R. p. 2928.
44 Ibid.
45 Ibid., p. 3179.
46 Ibid., p. 2900.
47 This was recommended in 1984 by the House of Lords Select Committee on the European Community: *18th Report, Commission's Powers of Investigation and Inspection*, HL, Session 1983–84, HMSO, para 45.
48 By Advocate General Mischo, in Cases 46/87 and 227/88, (1989) E.C.R., pp. 2900–1.
49 BverfG, E 51, p. 97, 107.
50 Ordonnance 86/1243, 1.12.86.
51 See generally the discussion by Advocate General Mischo in *Hoechst*, (1989) E.C.R., p. 2886 *et seq.*
52 (1989) E.C.R., p. 2926.
53 (1980) E.C.R., p. 2069.

4 Hearings: procedures and rights of defence

In the admittedly limited number of cases in which the Commission carries out an investigation, the result will almost certainly be a formal process of prosecution, in which the party or parties concerned must have the opportunity to present a defence before the Commission comes to a decision. The term 'hearing' in the context of Community competition proceedings is therefore in some respects analogous to the trial stage of the more familiar criminal law process, and enables the Commission's legal and evidential position to be tested by the other party, although of course in the Community procedure the Commission acts as both prosecutor and judge. The Commission's crucial role is subject to the possibility of subsequent review by the Court of Justice (and the Commission will be aware that such review may be rigorous) and also to the more recently introduced supervision of the Hearing Officer, whose function is to ensure fair play at the time of the hearing. In this discussion, the term 'hearing' will be used to encompass the process beginning with the opening of a formal procedure, and followed then by the statement of objections made by the Commission, the response by the 'defending' parties, and finally the Commission's decision, although the content of such decisions, in terms of orders and sanctions, will be dealt with at a later stage. The relevant analogies in national criminal procedure are to be found in the acts of laying a charge, prosecuting a case and determining liability.

The opening of proceedings

There is a clear distinction between the business of receiving complaints and information and carrying out investigations, on the one hand, and that of initiating a procedure against a party for breach of the competition rules, on the other hand. The latter, as the first formal step directed at establishing a breach by a particular party, necessarily activates rights of defence for such a party, who may fairly be then described as a 'defendant', or defending party. The 'initiation' of a procedure is thus something like the process of being charged with a criminal offence, although without the specifically accusatorial character of a 'charge'. But it serves to give notice to the party concerned that it is in a defending position.

In fact, it is by comparing the 'initiation of a procedure' with the idea of charging someone with an offence that the indeterminate nature of the former becomes more evident. The 'initiation' is nowhere defined in Community legislation; there is only a reference in Article 9(3) of Regulation 17 to 'initiating a procedure' under Articles 2, 3 or 6 of the Regulation, that is to say, a procedure to determine whether or not there has been a breach of the competition rules. The initiation of proceedings does not have to take a particular form. The Court of Justice has stated that the act referred to in Article 9(3) was 'obviously ... an authoritative act of the Commission, evidencing its intention of taking a decision'.[1] Any earlier receipt or collection of information does not therefore constitute the opening of proceedings, and the use of the German term *einleiten* and the French *engager* in Article 9(3) both confirm this. Although 'authoritative', there is no strict requirement for a formally recorded act[2] and it is not a 'decision' the legality of which may be challenged under Article 173 of the Treaty;[3] but for obvious practical reasons the Commission will have a formal record. The Commissioner responsible for competition matters, acting in the name of the Commission as a whole, will sign a form declaring that proceedings have been opened. The date of this formal act is then crucial for purposes of barring any proceedings relating to the same matter by Member State authorities, as laid down in Article 9(3) of Regulation 17.

The parties concerned, and any relevant Member State authorities, will be informed, but this need not be done immediately.[4] On the other hand, calculation of the time-limits within which the Commission must reach a decision, under Regulation 2988/74, is made from the date of communication to the parties of the decision to open proceedings. But neither will failure to notify the parties straightaway prejudice any rights of defence; these cannot meaningfully be exercised until the defending parties know the case against them, as laid down in the statement of objections, so that it is the issue of the latter which is important in that respect. It is also important to remember that the decision to open proceedings is essentially an exercise of discretion: prosecution is necessarily selective, both in view of the Commission's limited resources,[5] and possible difficulties of law and evidence.

The cumbrous and portentous nature of the official act opening proceedings helps to explain why it is usually left to a later moment in the overall procedure. The Commission will not wish to take formal action until it is sure of its case, and this may require careful investigation beforehand. Fact-gathering powers may therefore be exercised, to the knowledge of the parties concerned or not, well in advance of the latter knowing for certain that they are the subject of formal proceedings. Indeed, the Court of Justice has stated that it is not even necessary to know of the initiation of proceedings before the statement of objections is received.[6] At the other extreme, it has been asserted[7] that no investigation should be carried out before proceedings have been formally opened, on the ground that the serious nature of such proceedings should activate rights of defence at the earliest possible opportunity. Against this view, however, it may be argued that comparable powers exist at the national level in relation to economic offences;[8] that the position of complainants may be further prejudiced by such early warning to potential defendants; and, most importantly, that it is difficult to see how rights of defence are seriously injured, unless it be to admit the right to destroy incriminating evidence through early warning, which view is unlikely to command much support. There is a strong practical and moral argument that, in any system of formal investigation, the prosecuting authority must be allowed to prepare it ground effectively before opening a procedure, and this would include the ability to determine whether or not there is a serious case to answer.

Rights of defence

Despite the official characterisation of the hearing as an 'administrative' procedure and the official denial that the Commission acts as a tribunal, important rights of defence are necessarily conceded during the hearing. The formal description of the Commission's procedure has a number of consequences. Firstly, it is asserted that the Commission cannot be regarded as a tribunal susceptible of control under Article 6 of the European Convention on Human Rights. The Court of Justice has clearly affirmed that view,[9] although it should at the same time be borne in mind that the European Court of Human Rights has stated in its *Ozturk* judgement[10] that the description of proceedings is not decisive for this purpose; it is their substantive character that is crucial. The *Ozturk* case itself was concerned with minor road traffic offences characterised as 'administrative' under German law, but the Court's comments were of general application. The applicability of Article 6 of the Convention to Community competition proceedings has yet to be finally tested therefore, since it is the Court of Human Rights that has jurisdiction to determine that issue, and the assertions by the Court of Justice need to be treated with some caution.

In the second place, the categorisation as an administrative procedure can be used to justify the concentration of functions of prosecution, investigation and decision-making in one body. As has been noted, there had originally been a separation of personnel within the Commission as between the investigation and other parts of the procedure, a point relied upon by the Commission in its defence in the *AM&S Europe* case.[11] In 1984, however, DG IV was reorganised so as to allow a number of teams of officials to specialise in particular economic sectors[12] and since then the same personnel would be involved in both the investigation and in the later stages of a case concerned with an alleged breach of the competition rules. This reorganisation provoked some criticism, for instance, from the U.K. House of Lords Select Committee on the European Communities,[13] and in the European Parliament. The latter, in its Resolution on the Commission's *Fourteenth Report on Competition Policy*[14] stated that the Commission should:

> again examine whether it would not be preferable to distinguish clearly between the position of investigating official (inspector) and that of prosecutor (grievances), as was the case before the recent reorganization.

The Commission responded to these concerns in its *Fifteenth Report*[15] by giving reassurance about its respect for due process. It argued that this was achieved through both a recently established administrative unit for the 'coordination of competition decisions', which provides a separate assessment of each case at a number of stages in the procedure (though it does not deal with the investigation phase) and via the scrutiny of the Hearing Officer. Ultimately, however, the sanction for due process resides in the possibility of judicial review, and the Commission's legal service is likely to be alert to this prospect, since practice has shown that it is real enough. The 'defendants' in the process are likely to be large companies with the resources and confidence to mount a legal challenge on procedural issues, sometimes almost as a matter of course. The character of the parties usually subject to these proceedings and the extent of their legal support thus in itself provides some kind of guarantee of regard for due process.

Rights of defence have been provided for at both the legislative and the judicial level. Regulation 99/63 supplies the framework in laying down the basic mechanisms: the statement of objections, the right to reply and the provision for oral hearings. This framework has been fleshed out in a rapidly expanding body of case law. There is no doubt, therefore, about the need to ensure basic procedural fairness, even in such an 'administrative' procedure, and what should be the Commission's attitude was usefully spelt out by Advocate General Slynn:

> Obviously the Commission must conduct the procedure leading up to the adoption of its decision fairly, addressing itself to the case with a mind open to all the evidence and all the arguments which may be put to it.[16]

It is this attitude of open-mindedness, implying a weighing of argument and evidence, which suggests that the Commission is, at the hearing stage, a tribunal of some kind, and no amount of terminology should be allowed to obscure that fact.

The statement of objections (SO)[17]

This is the first main stage of the hearing, embodying the defending party's right to be informed of the Commission's case, or 'charge'. The SO is provided for in Article 2(1) of Regulation 99:

> The Commission shall inform undertakings and associations of undertakings in writing of the objections raised against them. The communication shall be addressed to each of them or to a joint agent appointed by them.

The SO must therefore be in writing and effectively communicated – the option of indirect communication by publication in the Official Journal, laid down in Article 2(2), has not so far been used. In essence, the SO is a summary of the Commission's case against the party(ies), containing crucial facts and legal argument, with some indication of supporting evidence, for purposes of both the substance of the Commission's ultimate decision and any proposed fine. It need not be a complete and detailed account of the Commission's case. The formula repeatedly used by the Court in this respect is that the statement is sufficient if it sets out clearly, albeit succinctly, the essential facts on which the Commission relies. The important point is that the parties must understand the nature of the case against them and the evidence on which the Commission has built its case.[18]

The SO must also indicate the time within which the party(ies) should make any defence (Article 2(4) of Regulation 99). Under Article 11(1) of the Regulation, this period, calculated from the date of receipt of the SO, must be at least two weeks and the length of time given should depend on two factors: the time necessary to prepare comments (in practice, this means the complexity of the case); and its urgency. In the natural course of events, such proceedings are likely to involve serious infringements and probably difficult issues of evidence and law. This will be so, for instance, in cases alleging an abuse of a dominant position, or a concerted practice. On the other hand, once proven, there may not be much to say about a blatant export ban, but in such cases the parties may be tempted to construct procedural complaints to put forward in mitigation. Two or three months would seem to be the norm. The Commission was subject to strong criticism in the *Commercial Solvents* case[19] for allowing only the minimum period to the parties to make their defence. In the view of Advocate General Warner, this was 'patently unreasonable' for a case of some complexity under Article 86. The Commission justified itself by pointing to the need for urgent intervention: the complainant in this case had been denied essential supplies of raw materials by the defendant parties. However, the Commission itself had been initially slow to take up the matter after the first complaint, and the Advocate General argued: 'If matters were urgent, it was for the Commission to hasten its own consideration of the case, not to adopt an improper procedure'[20] Partly for this reason, the Court of Justice subsequently reduced the amount of the fine. In later cases, the Commission has allowed periods of several months if the issues have been complex, and may also allow extensions.[21]

The SO must also append any documents relied upon by the Commission as evidence, so as to enable the party(ies) to consider their probative value.

This is an important element in the effective exercise of a right of defence and the Commission must be careful how it uses any discretion to omit documents from any list attached to the statement. So, for instance, the fact that documents were provided by the defending party itself is no good reason to exclude reference to them, since the defending party needs to know whether the Commission intends to rely upon such documents or considers them to be of any importance. What is important is not the documents as such, but the conclusions which the Commission has drawn from them.[22] As another example, in the *Distillers* case,[23] the Commission considered that information in a communication from a complainant was not relevant to the case it was putting forward and so left it out of the SO. Advocate General Warner accepted Distillers' argument that the company was thereby disadvantaged, since it was unable to refute erroneous information which, though not used as evidence, may have created an unfavourable impression. Nor was it able to use some of that information which in fact supported its own position.[24] (However, this was no more than a 'rap on the knuckles'; neither the Advocate General nor the Court considered that this procedural irregularity should vitiate the Commission's decision as a whole.)[25] Such arguments indicate the need for a scrupulous approach by the Commission in supplying relevant documentary evidence to the defending party.

The defending party's response

This should be made in writing within the time stipulated in the SO (Article 3 of Regulation 99). The written nature of the procedure may contribute to its 'administrative' designation; however, the evidential and procedural niceties also suggest a judicial quality.

At this stage the defending party may introduce contradictory evidence, either in documentary form or by naming witnesses who may corroborate facts asserted by the defending party (Article 11(3)). This part of the procedure may develop into an exchange of argument or evidence and the Commission may communicate fresh evidence to the defending party if such comes to light. If any new evidence substantially changes the thrust of the Commission's case, it may be necessary to issue a second or supplementary SO. However, in a number of cases a new SO seems to have been regarded as unnecessary if the defending party is given sufficient opportunity to consider the evidence in question.[26]

It is also at this stage that some kind of settlement or informal agreement may be reached, either in place of a formal decision by the Commission or in anticipation of its decision. The practice of informal settlement will be considered later (see Ch. 6), but it may be noted for the present that processes analogous to out-of-court settlement and plea-bargaining do in effect operate within the context of the Commission's procedure, once again underlining the judicial character of the adoption of a formal decision by the Commission.

The procedure at this stage is not only a dialogue between the Commission and the defending party; interested third parties must be given the opportunity to make known their views (Article 19(2) of Regulation 17; Article 7 of Regulation 99). Other parties with a 'sufficient interest' should be able to comment in writing within time-limits set down by the Commission (Article 5, Regulation 99). In practice such a third party may well be a complainant (in which case the procedure is an acknowledgement of 'victim's' rights) and the Commission will usually provide complainants with the substance of the SO and the defending party's response,[27] although this is not an entitlement. The Commission's approach to the question of 'sufficient interest' may be flexible: on one occasion it allowed a complainant to make submissions in writing while reserving its position on the question of whether the latter had such an interest.[28] Generally, however, a complainant would be regarded as a sufficiently interested party, and this is certainly true of Member State governments who are minded to intervene.

Oral hearings

Although the procedure is based on the expectation that it will be primarily in written form (as befits an 'administrative' proceeding), provision was also made for oral hearings when necessary (Article 19, Regulation 17; Article 7(1), Regulation 99). The defending party, or an interested third party, needs to take the initiative in requesting an oral hearing; but if the Commission is proposing to impose a fine or a periodic penalty payment, the party concerned will be entitled to a hearing upon request. It should be emphasised that the oral stage is a supplementary proceeding, not the culmination of the Commission's procedure and should not be thought of in terms of a conventional court hearing under national law. As Advocate General Roemer stated:

> ... the purpose of the oral hearing is the completion and explanation of written arguments and ... where the written comments are very detailed, the hearing itself can take place in a shortened form.[29]

Hearings rarely last for more than a day,[30] are not open to the public (Article 9(3) of Regulation 99), and the parties being heard may be called in separately (Article 9(3)), although the Commission's preferred practice seems to be to hear the defending parties and complainant's in each others' presence, except when confidential information is being discussed. Member States may send representatives to the hearings (Article 8(2)). The procedure is largely inquisitorial, consisting principally of a series of statements, starting with an introduction by the Commission's rapporteur and followed by presentations by the parties and any witnesses; questions may be asked by either Commission or Member State representatives. The parties who appear before a hearing may be legally represented (Article 9(2)) and must verify the record of any statements made by themselves (Article 9(4)). The purpose of the hearing is very much that of a final inquiry designed to confirm and clarify and if need be supplement the evidence and arguments brought forward at the written stage.

Nonetheless, it is possible to see some potential for adversarial discourse in the oral hearing. This springs from the Commission's practice of hearing the parties together so that there is some opportunity, if not for cross-examination, then at least to take up points made by the other parties (adequate rights of defence require the opportunity to challenge any such fresh points). Evidence can be tested by corroboration and by expert opinion. Moreover, the role of the Hearing Officer, introduced in 1982, to ensure fair procedure and respect for the rights of defence, is suggestive of dialogue rather than mere collection and verification of evidence. The Hearing Officer organises and chairs the hearings and produces a separate report on the proceeding.[31] Indeed, since the post was established in response to allegations of lack of due process, the role of this official suggests a 'judicialisation' of the procedure, with an emphasis on the opportunity to challenge the argument and evidence put forward by other parties. Nevertheless, there is no hard-and-fast dividing line between administrative and judicial process and the Commission's hearings have an evolutionary character, still lacking some of the common characteristics of a national court proceeding, such as a power to order attendance, or require answers to questions, or the use of sworn evidence ('summoning' persons to attend, under Article 9(2) of Regulation 99, in fact means 'inviting').[32]

Adoption of the decision

When the process of 'hearing', in the wider sense, has been completed, the Commission will draft its final decision. However, before adopting the formal decision, the draft, together with the most important documentary evidence (probably including the minutes of the oral hearing)[33] must be placed before the Advisory Committee on Restrictive Practices and Monopolies for its opinion (see Articles 10, 15 and 16 of Regulation 17). This representative body is made up of officials from the Member States who are competent in competition questions (for instance, from the U.K. Office of Fair Trading or the German Bundeskartellamt). Its opinion is in no way binding upon the Commission but is not disclosed to anybody else. It is therefore difficult to assess the impact of this Committee's views, but it is clear that it can at that stage only influence the Commission through the *assessment* of established evidence and argument. It could, for example, perhaps be persuasive as regards the amount of a fine proposed by the Commission, or in judging the seriousness of a breach. Regulation 17 is categorical about the non-disclosure of the opinion (Article 10(6), for instance: 'It shall not be made public') and the Court of Justice has ruled that the opinion cannot be disclosed confidentially to the undertakings, even if directly concerned by it.[34]

It has been questioned whether this position is consistent with the parties' rights of defence. In the *Distillers* case,[35] Advocate General Warner expressed doubts. He viewed the Advisory Committee procedure:

> with unease, because of the secrecy which surrounds it. The undertakings concerned are left in the dark as to what the Committee is told or not told by the Commission and as to the content of the Committee's report. They have no opportunity of addressing the Committee.[36]

This kind of debate begs the question of the Advisory Committee's function. Since it is clearly not to review the Commission's decision, it may be doubted whether it is strictly necessary for the parties to have access to the Committee's opinion (and this was the Court of Justice's view in *Musique Diffusion Francaise*).[37] What is implied in the Court's judgement in that case is that the opinion of the Committee does not materially affect the outcome of individual cases. If, then, the Committee's role is to maintain in a general way an overview of the Commission's decision making and to keep the Commission in touch with thinking at the Member State level, can it be necessary to insist on such secrecy, which may in itself be a source of disquiet? What is unsettling about this state of affairs is that it is not clear how influential the Committee may be; there is only the Court's presumption that the Commission cannot rely ultimately on the Committee's opinion since the parties are not allowed to comment on it. If this is true, what is the real value and role of the Committee's opinion and why should it be shrouded in secrecy?

Once the Committee has given its opinion, the Commission may proceed to adopt its decision formally. Formal decisions must be communicated to the parties concerned and any decision ordering termination of an infringement must be published (Article 21 of Regulation 17). In practice, the Commission also publishes decisions imposing fines, and sometimes issues press releases. It is possible for a press statement to pre-date the receipt of the full text of the decision by the defending party, and this has been properly criticised. In 1982 the Association Nationale des Services d'Eau Asbl (ANSEAU) complained[38] in proceedings before the Court of Justice that as a result of a press release being issued a month before it received the full text of the Commission's decision, the Association and its members were referred to in the media while lacking the means (that is, the benefit of the Commission's reasoning) to defend themselves against media comment. However, Advocate General Verloren van Themaat pointed out the useful deterrent element inherent in such publicity: that such media attention may help to ensure observance of the competition rules.[39] The Court's tone was more critical, referring to such conduct on the Commission's part as 'regrettable', but indicating at the same time that such subsequent behaviour on the part of the Commission cannot affect the validity of a decision already adopted.[40]

It is quite clear that any published text must respect the confidentiality of any information in the Commission's possession. Article 21(2) of Regulation 17 states that publication 'shall have regard to the legitimate interests of undertakings in the protection of their business secrets'.

Notes

1 Case 48/72, *Brasserie de Haecht v Wilkin (No. 2)* (1973) E.C.R. 77.
2 Advocate General Mayras in Case 127/83, *BRT v SABAM* (1974) E.C.R. 51, p. 71.
3 Case 60/81, *IBM v Commission* (1981) E.C.R. 1857.
4 Case 48/69, *ICI v Commission* (1972) E.C.R. 619.
5 See Ian Forrester and Christopher Norall , 'The Laicization of Community Law: Self-Help and the Rule of Reason – How Competition Law is and could be Applied', 21 (1984) C.M.L.Rev. 11.
6 Case 48/69, see note 4 above, (1972) E.C.R., p. 650.
7 Sedemund, Vaughn and Hall, referred to in P.J. Kuyper and T.P.J.N. van Rijn, 'Procedural Guarantees and Investigatory Methods in European Law, 2 (1982) *Yearbook of European Law*, p. 12.
8 Kuyper and van Rijn, op. cit., p. 12.
9 Cases 209–215, 218/78, *Van Landewyck v Commission* (1980) E.C.R. 3125; Cases 100–103/80, *Musique Diffusion Francaise v Commission* (1983) E.C.R. 1825, 1880.
10 *Ozturk v Germany* (1984) 6 *European Human Rights Reports* 409.
11 Case 155/79, *AM & S Europe* (1982) E.C.R. 1593.
12 Christopher Bellamy and Graham Child, *Common Market Law of Competition*, (3rd ed., 1987), p. 22; see Chapter 2 in this volume.
13 House of Lords, Select Committee, *Eighth Report, Competition Practice*
14 O.J. 1985, C345, point 46.
15 *Fifteenth Report on Competition Policy* (1985), point 45.
16 Case 86/82, *Hasselblad v Commission* (1984) E.C.R. 883, 915.
17 Referred to as 'notice of objections' in some earlier cases.
18 See Cases 45/69 and 17/74, *Transocean Marine Paint Association v Commission* (1974) E.C.R. 1063.
19 Cases 6 and 7/73, *Commercial Solvents v Commission* (1974) E.C.R. 223.
20 Ibid., p. 275.
21 See, for example, Case 60/81, *IBM v Commission* (1981) E.C.R. 1857.
22 Case 107/82, *AEG v Commission* (1983) E.C.R. 3151, 3193.
23 Case 30/78, *Distillers v Commission* (1980) E.C.R. 2229.
24 Ibid., p. 2295 *et seq*.
25 Ibid., p. 2264 and p. 2298.
26 Cases 209/78 etc, *van Landerwyck v Commission* (1980) E.C.R. 3125; Cases 100/80 etc, *Musique Diffusion Francaise v Commission* (1983) E.C.R. 1825.
27 Commission, *Thirteenth Report on Competition Policy* (1983), point 74(b).
28 Case 8/71, *Deutscher Kompanistenverband v Commission* (1971) E.C.R. 705.
29 Advocate General Roemer in Case 6/72, *Continental Can v Commission* (1973) E.C.R., p. 264.
30 Ferry, 'Procedure and Powers of the EEC Commission in Antitrust Cases', (1979) *European Intellectual Property Review* 126.

31 Commission, *Thirteenth Report on Competition Policy* (1983), p. 273.
32 Cf as well the Court's downplaying of any 'adversarial' features in the Commission's procedure, in Cases 142 and 156/84, *BAT and R.J, Reynolds v Commission* (1987) E.C.R. 4487; also discussed in Chapter 6 in this volume.
33 Advocate General Warner, in Case 30/78, *Distillers v Commission* (1980) E.C.R. 2229, p. 2294.
34 Case 100/80 etc., referred to in note 26, above, (1983) E.C.R. p. 1886.
35 Case 30/78, see note 33 above, p. 2229.
36 Ibid., p. 2292.
37 See cases referred to in note 26, above, (1983) E.C.R. 1887.
38 Cases 96/82 etc, *IAZ v Commission* (1983) E.C.R. 3369.
39 Ibid., p. 3425.
40 Ibid., p. 3409.

5 The role of third parties

As the Commission's practice, and the Court of Justice's review of this practice has evolved, the role of third parties – especially when these are complainants – has become increasingly important. By its nature, anti-competitive behaviour is not especially visible or obvious and this distinguishes it from many other forms of objectionable conduct, especially classical criminal offences. Traditional property offences, for example, often have a clear physical manifestation. The area of fraud provides a closer analogy with anti-competitive behaviour, in its covert, technical and often economically complex forms.[1] In the case of both sophisticated fraud and restrictive market behaviour, investigation and identification of the offending conduct can be very problematical and much may depend upon the matter being brought to light by those adversely affected by it: victim-complainants may therefore play a crucial role. Consideration of the complainant's position gives rise to a number of legal issues, most importantly the protection of the complainant's own interests (which often resolves itself into a question of confidential treatment), and the opportunity for the complainant to participate in the legal assessment of the case and to challenge the defending party's arguments or evidence.

On the other hand, some third parties may not be hostile to the defending undertaking and may wish to lend support to its defence. Some traders, for instance, members of a selective distribution system, may benefit from the impugned practice and wish to intervene in its favour. Member State governments may also wish to 'appear' for the defence. The right to be heard, on the basis of a 'sufficient interest', has therefore assumed significance and allows for a fuller consideration of both evidence and argument in the Commission's decision-making process.

It may be useful to analyse the role of third parties with reference to a number of rights accorded to them in relation to Community investigations and hearings: the right of complaint; the right of protection (often, in practice, a right of confidentiality, which itself then impinges on the defending party's right of access to the Commission's file); the right to be heard; and the right to challenge the rejection of a complaint by the Commission.

The right of complaint

As already noted, complaints are an important element in the effective enforcement of competition policy, especially in relation to the more covert and sophisticated practices entered into by large and experienced companies. The number of complaints made to the Commission in recent years can be seen from Table 5.1:

Table 5.1 Complaints made to the Commission in the period 1983–1987

	complaints made	complaints pending
1983	56	283
1984	76	314
1985	66	296
1986	75	330
1987	93	344

Source: Commission, annual *Reports on Competition Policy.*

This represents a general increase in the number of complaints during the 1980s, with the Commission's backlog at least remaining in proportion to that increased level of complaints.

There are few formalities in relation to the submission of a complaint: an ordinary letter will suffice, although there is an official Form C that may be used (complaints should be distinguished from the provision of information, allowing the Commission then to act 'on its own initiative', as in *Hoffmann-la Roche*).[2] Under Article 10(1) of Regulation 17, copies of all complaints must be sent on to the relevant Member State authorities.

The main issue concerned with the making of a complaint arises from the requirement under Article 3(2) of Regulation 17 that it be made by a natural or legal person with a 'legitimate interest'. This has been interpreted by commentators in a commonsense way as a 'reasonably direct and practical interest'[3] or more narrowly as 'likely to suffer injury or loss directly'.[4] What seems to be important in practice is the existence of an actual personal interest as opposed to concern which is theoretical or speculative. As regards engaging the Commission's interest and moving it to act, it is not really an important issue since the Commission can proceed 'on its own initiative' if there is substance in the complaint.[5] The complainant's interest is likely to have greater practical significance in relation to its right to participate in the hearing.

In practice complainants are usually affected by the alleged restrictive practice in a clear way: typical categories of complainant include traders or consumers affected by export bans, competing manufacturers, traders excluded from distribution schemes, traders denied access to supplies, and licensees or members of trading associations subject to restrictive obligations.[6] Representative bodies, such as trade unions or consumer organisations, may well have a sufficient interest;[7] not surprisingly, therefore, a trade union alleging a concerted practice to close down an oil refinery would be considered to have a real interest in the matter on behalf of its members likely to be made redundant by that action.[8]

Problems may arise if, having received a complaint, the Commission decides to take no action without any further examination of the matter. In the *Demo-Studio Schmidt* case,[9] a trader excluded from a selective distribution scheme for audio-visual goods complained about this to the Commission, who took a decision not to act upon the complaint. The Court of Justice stated that:

> the Commission, having received the applicant's complaint, was under a duty to examine the facts put forward by the applicant in order to decide whether Revox's application of its selective distribution system was capable of distorting competition.[10]

It would seem, then, that the Commission's general duty to ensure application of the competition rules would include proper examination of a complaint, certainly when that complaint has been submitted by a party with a genuine interest in the matter. On the other hand, the Commission is entitled, after an initial investigation, to decide that the complaint is not well-founded (this may be, for example, for lack of evidence, or because the offending conduct has been amended). In such a case the Commission should, under Article 6 of Regulation 99 of 1963, set out in writing its reasons for not acting further on the complaint and allowing the complainant to submit any written comments within a certain time.

The right of protection

Usually complainants do not put themselves at risk by making a complaint to the Commission. On the contrary, they may have much to gain if their position is already adversely affected. If the Commisson acts upon the complaint, a powerful legal process is under way at no cost to the party who has complained. But in some cases certain interests of the complaining party may be at risk, and this gives rise to issues of legal protection. The main problems to be considered in this context comprise the protection of business secrets; the need not to disclose the party's identity; and the need for interim protection.

Protection of business secrets

This topic needs to be viewed in the wider context of the general need for confidentiality during the Commission's procedure. The question of confidential communications between lawyer and client has already been considered in the context of investigations, but the issue of confidential treatment arises at a number of points in relation both to the defending party and to third persons. The Commission is enjoined to respect confidence by a number of basic provisions. Article 214 of the EEC Treaty provides, in the first place:

> The members of the institutions of the Community, the members of committees, and the officials and other servants of the Community shall be required, even after their duties have ceased, not to disclose information of the kind covered by the obligation of professional secrecy, in particular information about undertakings, their business relations or their cost components.

Article 20(2) of Regulation 17 repeats the need to respect this obligation of professional secrecy, stating that:

> the Commission and the competent authorities of the Member States, their officials and other servants shall not disclose information acquired by them as a result of the application of this Regulation and of the kind covered by the obligation of professional secrecy.

Moreover, Article 21(2) states that the publication of any decision taken by the Commission 'shall have regard to the legitimate interest of undertakings in the protection of their business secrets'. Article 9(3) of Regulation 99 repeats the same formula in relation to hearings when parties are not dealt with separately. It is therefore clear that all parties may invoke a general right to respect confidentiality.

How far this right extends is less certain, however.[11] In the context of the Commission's procedure, apart from the question of lawyer-client communications, the main issue would seem to involve 'business secrets', a particular category of confidential information. The term 'business secret' does not have a clear legal definition and in practice may encompass a range of information, including technical information and know-how on the one hand and, on the other hand and more relevantly, business information relating to costs, market share, turnover, sales plans and forecasts, and details of contracts. It is difficult to be categorical and it is a question of fact, related to the circumstances, whether or not information comprises such business secrets. One argument is that the test of secrecy should depend upon whether a revelation of the information would harm the interests of the party concerned; since such harm in most cases is likely to mean damage to competitive position, this whole issue could be productive of a good deal of inconclusive debate. Another approach would be to accept that a case for secrecy can be made if the information is not generally accessible through legitimate means. This would be easier to prove and would seem to be the position implicitly favoured by the Court of Justice. For instance, the Court has ruled that the divulgence of information to other parties in confidence would not deprive that information of its secret character, if it still has restricted access.[12] But even in that judgement the Court was talking about 'information in the nature of a trade secret',[13] which begs the question as to what is in the nature of a trade secret in the first place. The Advocate General in that case, Advocate General Reischl, was unwilling to accept the party's own labelling of the information as secret; he considered that it should depend on the content of the information and that it could be regarded as secret if 'it is not possible to avoid the impression that it was a question of matters which ought not to have been brought in full detail to the knowledge of customers'.[14] But this kind of reasoning is impressionistic and subjective; in order to achieve some consistency, a more objective test of restricted access, whether for convincing reasons or not, should be preferred.

Leaving aside the problem of what qualifies in a particular case as business secrets, there are two main principles which flow from the recognition of the interests in confidentiality as regards such secrets. The first is that the Commission should respect the confidential character of such information and not divulge it to any other party. including of course other parties involved in the proceedings. The second principle follows from the first: that if another party in the proceedings cannot be told about such information and cannot therefore challenge its probative value, then it should not be used against that other person. This may therefore restrict the Commission's ability to use certain evidence, if it may not be subject to cross-examination.

The principle of non-disclosure of business secrets was discussed by the Court of Justice in the *AKZO* case.[15] During a proceeding relating to the chemical manufacturer AKZO in 1984, the Commission had communicated certain documents to the complaining party without telling AKZO that it had done so. AKZO maintained that some of this information comprised business secrets and that it had been given no opportunity to challenge the Commission's proposed communication of the documents. The Court emphasised that business secrets are afforded special protection; there was a risk otherwise that companies might be tempted to lodge a complaint with the Commission solely in order to gain access to competitors' business secrets.[16] But, while such documents should not therefore be forwarded to complainants, it is for the Commission to decide whether or not specific information amounts to a business secret. In deciding this issue, the Commission should follow a certain procedure: it must allow the party concerned to state its views on the matter, it must then adopt a reasoned decision, and this decision must be challengeable before the Court of Justice, so that the latter can review the Commission's assessment before any documents are passed over.[17] Clearly nothing like that had been done in AKZO's case. If any information is communicated to other parties, such as complainants, it cannot be used for any purposes outside of the Commission's proceedings (Article 20(1) of Regulation 17). So, for example, it could not be used in proceedings before a national court or during an investigation by Member State competition authorities. In summary, then, it may be said that business secrets (as determined by the Commission under the procedure laid down in *AKZO*) are sacrosanct; other information, even if of a more broadly confidential nature, may be supplied to third parties so that they may exercise their rights to be heard, but on a *confidential* basis, and may not be used elsewhere.

Problems have also arisen in connection with the second principle, in cases where a defending party has challenged the Commission's reliance on evidence being used against that party, when the latter has not been able to test it on account of its confidential nature. The guiding principle on this issue was stated by the Court of Justice in the *Hoffmann-la Roche* case.[18] The Court stated that the essence of the problem was to reconcile the right of confidentiality, as laid down in both the Treaty and in regulations, with the rights of defence. The Commission had received data from competitors and customers of Roche which it then used in its calculation of market shares and in order to form the view that the company's behaviour was abusive under Article 86 of the Treaty. But, in order to respect the confidential character of this information (as business secrets), it refused to give Roche access to it. The Court stated, as a matter of principle, that the Commission could not be allowed to use

> to the detriment of the undertakings involved in a proceeding referred to in Regulation 17, facts, circumstances or documents which it cannot in its view disclose if such a refusal of disclosure adversely affects that undertaking's opportunity to make known effectively its views on the truth or implications of those circumstances, on those documents or again on the conclusions drawn by the Commission from them.[19]

Indeed, in the case of Hoffman-la Roche, the Court concluded that Roche had been able to make known its views on the evidence in question. One way around the problem of squaring the duty of non-disclosure with respect for the rights of defence is to provide other parties with a non-confidential summary of a confidential document.[20] This may still, however, not fully resolve the issue: the question may still arise as to whether the other party is able properly to challenge the reliability of original confidential information through such a summary.

Non-disclosure of identity

Returning now to the more specific issue of the complainant's interests which may require legal protection, there next arises the related problem of confidential treatment of a complainant or informant's identity. In many cases of complaint, this will not be an issue: complainant and defending party may well be in an open and declared relation of antagonism. In some situations, however, a complainant may fear the imposition of short-term but damaging

reprisals when the fact of the complaint is made known to the defending party
– for instance, the cutting off of essential supplies or the imposition of
intolerable trading conditions. In that kind of situation the most sensible
solution may involve the provision of interim relief or protection against such
measures. On the other hand, the danger may come from another source, as
was vividly illustrated by the Stanley Adams case.[21] Adams, a disenchanted
high-ranking employee of the Swiss pharmaceuticals company Hoffmann-la
Roche, provided the Commission with important information about the
firm's practice of using loyalty rebates as a means of holding potential
competitors at bay (an activity subsequently affirmed as a breach of Article 86
of the Treaty).[22] Adams had little to fear directly from the company since he
left its employment at the same time, but for understandable reasons preferred
not to have his identity as a 'whistle-blower' made known. During the ensuing
proceedings, however, the Commission's officials did not exercise sufficient
care to prevent his identity being worked out by Hoffmann-la Roche, and on
a later ill-judged visit to Switzerland, Adams was arrested and charged by the
Swiss authorities with offences of industrial espionage under Swiss law
(disclosure of business information contrary to Article 273 of the Swiss Penal
Code), with devastating personal consequences, including his wife's suicide.[23]
Adams subsequently claimed damages against the Commission under Article
215(2) of the Treaty, for injury resulting from the negligent disclosure of his
identity.

Adams' claim rested very much on the duty of confidentiality, based on
Article 214 of the Treaty, which he argued the Commission had breached. The
Court of Justice affirmed in its judgement[24] that in such circumstances an
informant is owed an obligation of confidentiality, that is, when information
is supplied voluntarily with a request for anonymity. Such an obligation
would not be terminated by the informant indicating that he would be willing
to appear before a court.[25] On the facts, the Court decided that the
Commission was under a duty to keep Adams' identity secret both before and
after he left Roche's employment. The breach of this obligation arose from the
Commission's action of showing to the company edited documents supplied
by Adams, in order to establish their authenticity, without taking sufficient
care to ensure that there was no way in which Adams' identity could be
deduced from even the edited versions of these documents. The breach was
compounded by the Commission's subsequent failure to warn Adams of the
risk that his identity might have been revealed.[26] The Court therefore
awarded damages against the Commission, but reduced the amount to take
into account Adams' own negligence in not fully informing the Commission
as to what methods Roche could use to trace his identity, and in not making
sufficient enquiry into the progress of Roche's own investigation and the risks
to himself therefrom. There had been, then, in the Court's view, a lack of
communication on both sides. (Interestingly, Advocate General Mancini, in
his opinion in the case, was less sympathetic to Adams' claim).[27]

The Adams case was also of significance in clearly demonstrating the sanctions which underlie a breach of confidence of this kind by the Commission's officials (an award of damages in that particular case). Commission officials could also be subject to disciplinary measures.[28] The Commission itself was forced to draw the lesson and establish guidelines of good practice in this area:

> Where the identity of the person providing the information is known to the Commission, the documents may be shown or returned to the firm concerned, within the limits indicated by that person, only after he has been warned of the various risks this may entail for him and on the strict condition that he has authorized the Commission to do so. Where, on the other hand, the author or sender of the documents has not revealed his identity, the documents will not be shown or returned to the firm until after a detailed examination by the Commission's staff of their importance to the investigation, the risk that they might be traced back to the person concerned and the possibility that he might be subjected to legal proceedings.[29]

Interim protection

Some third parties may consider that their position is already seriously affected in an adverse way by the act complained of and that irreparable harm could be suffered during the time taken by the Commission to come to a decision in the matter. Although interim relief against such damage is not provided for explicitly in Regulation 17, the Court of Justice has proved itself to be sensitive to this problem and ruled in 1980 in the *Camera Care* case that the Commission's powers under Article 3(1) of that Regulation extended to the award of such relief.[30] The essential conditions on which such measures must be based, were laid down in the following terms:

> ... it is esssential that interim measures be taken only in cases proved to be urgent in order to avoid a situation likely to cause serious and irreparable damage to the party seeking their adoption, or which is intolerable for the public interest. A further requirement is that these measures be of a temporary and conservatory nature and restricted to what is required in the given situation.[31]

This is another example of the Court taking a more adventurous approach than its Advocate General. In his opinion in *Camera Care*, Advocate General Warner was unwilling to interpret Article 3(1) so widely. He argued that:

> Article 3 is inconsistent with the Commission having power, before it has issued a decision based on a finding of infringement, to go further than to address recommendations to the undertakings concerned ... the necessary implication from the terms of ... Regulation [17] is that its authors had no intention of conferring such a power on the Commission. Whether they were right or wrong is not the question.[32]

In his view it was first of all necessary for the Council to authorise such powers. The Court took some of the Advocate General's points, however, in insisting that interim protection could only be based on a *prima facie* case of infringement being made out and stipulating that the parties affected by the order for interim measures be given an opportunity to be heard on the matter in accordance with Regulation 99, and that the Commission's decision should be reviewable by the Court.[33]

The *Camera Care* ruling arose out of the measures taken by the Swedish manufacturer of photographic equipment, Victor Hasselblad, to withhold direct and indirect supplies of its products to the British company Camera Care. The latter sought an interim decision from the Commission, to whom it had made a complaint, requiring Hasselblad to supply its products to Camera Care. In that particular case, following the Court's ruling, interim relief was not in fact granted, Camera Care not satisfying the conditions laid down by the Court. However, the Commission has subsequently made such orders requiring the resumption of supplies.[34] In the *AKZO* proceedings[35] the Commission ordered AKZO to refrain from discriminatory and predatory pricing designed to drive the British company ECS out of the market (for instance, it was ordered not to supply certain chemicals to any flour milling undertaking in the U.K. below certain stated prices). In other cases the imminent possibility of interim measures has persuaded companies to give an undertaking to do what otherwise might have been enforced by the Commission's decision. In 1985 a major manufacturer of nail guns – Hilti, based in Leichtenstein – formally undertook to terminate its practice of tying the supply of its cartridge magazines to that of its nails.[36] In the same year, the Ford motor company agreed to offer licences to competitors for the manufacture and sale of body panels for Ford vehicles, after an application had been made for interim measures to that effect.[37] It is clear from such cases that a range of prohibitory and mandatory action will be contemplated by the Commission in providing interim relief in this context. How quickly interim measures can be obtained depends upon the nature of the case: ten weeks from the date of the request in *AKZO*, for example; in *Hilti*, where the matter was dealt with informally, the period was less than three weeks.[38] The Commission is likely to attempt to assess the potential damage to both sides in this kind of situation – thus the party seeking the relief may be required to provide a guarantee against loss to the other party, if no infringement is subsequently established by the Commission, as was done in *NCB/National Smokeless Fuels/NCC*, a Coal and Steel Community case.[39]

It should be noted, in fact, that there is clear provision for such interim relief under the European Coal and Steel Community Treaty. Article 66(5) of that Treaty, for instance, empowers the Commission to 'take or cause to be taken such interim measures of protection as it may consider necessary ...'. So, in the *NCC* case the Court of Justice stated that it was appropriate for the Commission to take measures of conservation which were strictly necessary to keep in operation the NCC plants threatened with closure pending the Commission's final decision.[40] The provision of such powers under the Coal and Steel Treaty may have fortified the Court's resolve in *Camera Care* that they should be similarly available to the Commission in the context of EEC competition proceedings.

The right to be heard

It has already been noted in the previous chapter that third parties with a sufficient interest may present written and even oral observations during the Commission's written procedure.[41] Similarly, the mutual rights of access to information provided by the Commission to defending parties and complainants has already been discussed.[42] It remains to say something about the interest which must be shown by third parties in order to participate in the Commission's procedure. There seems little doubt in practice that a complainant would have a sufficient interest for this purpose, in view of the fact that third parties with a real, though less direct interest in the subject-matter of the complaint (for instance, traders *included* in a selective distribution scheme from which the complainant has been excluded)[43] have been clearly accepted by the Court of Justice as having a sufficient interest. The Court has confirmed that under Article 7(2) of Regulation 99 the Commission has a 'reasonable margin of discretion to decide how expedient it may be to hear persons whose evidence may be relevant to the enquiry'.[44] It seems that it is only persons with a very tenuous interest who would be excluded in the exercise of this discretion (in the *VBVB and VBBB* case, for instance, the President of the Flemish Literary Association in his capacity as a writer).[45]

Some argument has arisen, however, not so much about the complainant's right to be heard at the formal stages of the procedure (when the statement of objections is issued, at the oral hearing, or when the complaint is rejected), but as regards the right to participate in informal negotiations between the Commission and the defending party. In the *Philip Morris* case,[46] the two complainant companies (BAT and Reynolds) challenged the Commission's failure to keep them informed about negotiations which had taken place between itself and the defending parties (Rembrandt and Philip Morris), which eventually led to a negotiated settlement and the Commission closing its file on the case. More will be said about the process of negotiated settlement in the following chapter, but it can be noted for present that the Court was unwilling to see the possibility of such informal settlement jeopardised by the complainant's intervention. The Court stressed that:

... the administrative procedure provides, among other things, an opportunity for the companies concerned to bring the agreements or practices complained of into conformity with the rules laid down in the Treaty. For such a possibility to be a real one, the companies concerned and the Commission must be entitled to enter into confidential negotiations in order to determine what alterations will remove the cause for the Commission's objections.

Such a right would be imperilled if the complainant were to attend the negotiations or be kept informed of the progress made in order to submit their observations on the proposals put forward by one party or the other. The legitimate interests of the complainants are fully protected when they are informed of the outcome of the negotiations in the light of which the Commission proposes to close the proceedings.[47]

What is seen to be at stake here is the effective enforcement of competition policy through informal as well as formal processes and it is possible from this judgement as a whole to detect the Court's concern that the Commission's procedure should not take on too much of an adversary character, which would undermine the scope for flexibility in achieving negotiated rather than prosecuted outcomes.[48]

The right to challenge the rejection of a complaint

The right to have the action taken by the Commission following a complaint reviewed by the Court of Justice depends upon there being a reviewable act which can be challenged before the Court under Article 173 of the Treaty. Such a reviewable decision may take a number of forms.

The most usual situation is that in which the complaint has been *directly* rejected by means of a letter from the Commission to the complainant. If during the course of the administrative procedure the Commission decides that it is not going to take the matter any further – for example, on the ground that there is no real basis in the allegation of an infringement, or if the defending party has modified its arrangements to comply with the competition rules – it must, under Article 6 of Regulation 99, send a letter to the complainant informing the latter of its reasons for doing so. The complainant must be given a period of time within which to submit any further comments. Regulation 99 does not stipulate that the Commission has to take a final decision in the matter following the receipt of such comments, but it is normal practice to do so and this definitive letter refusing to take any further action may be appealed to the Court of Justice under Article 173. It does not matter whether the Commission's definitive refusal to proceed further is in the form of such a letter[49] or adopted as a formal decision,[50] since in either case it will constitute a reviewable act. Although not fully provided for under Regulation 99, this procedure is nonetheless at the present time relatively straightforward.

The second, less usual situation, where the complaint is indirectly rejected, is legally more complex and productive of argument. In this kind of case, the Commission has taken a formal decision in favour of the practice complained of, either to the effect that it is outside the scope of Article 85(1) or Article 86 (a negative clearance) or that it satisfies the conditions for exemption under Article 85(3). So, for example, in 1973 the German wholesaler, Metro, complained to the Commission about the selective distribution scheme operated by SABA, a manufacturer of electrical goods. Following the Commission's examination of SABA's arrangements, the latter agreed to certain modifications which would satisfy the requirements of Article 85[51] and at the end of 1975 the Commission adopted a formal decision approving SABA's scheme. Although Metro was also notified of the Commission's decision, it was not the formal addressee of that decision. Therefore, when the company wished to challenge its legality, the question arose whether it had sufficient interest, or more exactly whether it was directly and individually concerned by a decision addressed to another person within the meaning of Article 173(2) of the Treaty.[52] Both the Court of Justice and Advocate General Reischl were of the view that the concept of direct and individual concern should not be interpreted restrictively as it had been in the context of decisions addressed to Member States being challenged by third party individuals. The Court's judgement identifies succintly Metro's interest in the matter:

> ... the contested decision was adopted in particular as the result of a complaint submitted by Metro and ... it relates to the provisions of SABA's distribution system, on which SABA relies and continues to rely as against Metro in order to justify its refusal to sell to the latter or to appoint it as a wholesaler, and which the applicant had for this reason impugned in its complaint.
>
> It is in the interests of a satisfactory administration of justice and of the proper application of Articles 85 and 86 that natural or legal persons who are entitled, pursuant to Article 3(2)(b) of Reg No. 17, to request the Commission to find an infringement of Articles 85 and 86 should be able, if their request is not complied with either wholly or in part, to institute proceedings in order to protect their legitimate interests.[53]

The Court's judgement therefore places particular emphasis on the complainant's participation in the Commission's administrative procedure. Advocate General Reischl was prepared to accept an even wider test of interest, although it was not necessary to do so in this particular case, arguing that 'any person who by virtue of his occupation may qualify for a distributorship but is excluded therefrom by the approved system is entitled to bring proceedings'.[54] This would open up the right of review to a range of disappointed distributors, as opposed to parties who had actually complained to the Commission, but it is not clear that the Court would be willing to go that far. In the *Timex* case,[55] the Court stressed the applicant's significant role in the Commission's administrative procedure (it was at the origin of a complaint which led to the opening of an anti-dumping procedure, and its views were heard and were of significance in the course of that procedure). Then, in relation to the examination of state aids,[56] the Court stated that:

the same conclusions apply to undertakings which have played a comparable role in the procedure referred to in Article 93 of the EEC Treaty provided, however, that their position on the market is significantly affected by the aid which is the subject of the contested decision.[57]

A significant impact on market position was clear enough in both *Metro* and *Timex* and it may have been implicit in the Court's determination of significant interest in both those cases. In any case, the Court's statement in relation to state aids decisions would militate against any open-ended principle that any competitor or disappointed trader is able to challenge a decision not addressed to itself; some kind of participation in or at least connection with the preceding administrative procedure is probably necessary.[58]

The discussion of sufficient interest, especially in relation to impact on market position, was taken up again by Advocate General Mancini in the *Philip Morris* case,[59] which concerned the transfer of shareholdings as between major tobacco manufacturers. The South African Rembrandt company had transferred half the equity in Rothmans Tobacco to Philip Morris and it had been agreed that Rothmans would be managed on a joint basis. Two competing tobacco manufacturers – BAT (British American Tobacco) and Reynolds – complained to the Commission that this arrangement was in contravention of Articles 85 and 86; the Commission reacted quickly by enquiring into the agreement but subsequently negotiated a settlement with Rembrandt and Philip Morris, then informing the complainants that it intended to close the file on the case. BAT and Reynolds were given the opportunity to state their views on the amended agreement negotiated with the Commission; the two companies were still convinced that the agreement should be declared unlawful, but the Commission was unwilling to proceed any further and duly notified the companies that it had rejected their complaints. Leaving aside for the present the questions raised by this proceeding in relation to the process of negotiated settlement, some note should be taken of some of Advocate General Mancini's arguments about the position of BAT and Reynolds.

Rembrandt had objected to the admissibility of BAT and Reynold's appeal against the Commission's decision to reject their complaint to the Court of Justice, arguing that the rejection of the complaint referred to a determination by the Commission (the lawfulness of the amended agreement) which was of no direct concern to the complainants. The Advocate General was prepared to adopt a more radical approach to the question of interest by regarding the likely impact of the Commission's decision on the complainants as decisive:

> ... it seems to me that the position of a person who challenges the rejection of his complaint is no different from that of a person who brings an action against a negative clearance or the grant of an exemption, in other words against measures which, formally, are not of concern to him, but ... essentially entail the dismissal of his application ....

... I do not see why the existence of a complaint is sufficient to give rise to the right to bring proceedings against a refusal on the part of the administration; and it does not seem to me that, for that purpose, any decisive importance can be attributed to the more or less active role played by the undertaking in the course of the procedure prior to the action before the Court.[60]

The Advocate General therefore wished to distinguish between the interest necessary to make a complaint and that necessary to challenge the Commission's refusal to take further action; they are not necessarily the same in his view:

> In other words, a person who lodges a complaint under Article 3 has a right to bring an action against the express or implied measure rejecting it only where he claims that, so far as may be reasonably foreseen, that measure will cause him to incur a loss.[61]

This is a significantly different approach, downplaying the formal role of complainant. It would give BAT and Reynolds sufficient interest to challenge the Commission's action since they are the major competitors of Rothmans and Philip Morris in the Community cigarette market. There could, however, be other complainants who conceivably would not be able to demonstrate such a foreseeable impact on their market position (see, for instance, Advocate General Mancini's example of the tobacconist).[62] The Court did not find it necessary to decide in any way on these arguments, contenting itself by saying that the Commission's decision was clearly addressed to the applicants within the meaning of Article 173(2) and that was all that needed to be decided.[63] It remains to be seen whether Advocate General Mancini's impatience with the terminological niceties of Article 173 will command any support in the future.

Notes

1 On comparisons between fraud and anti-competitive activity, see Michael Levi, 'Developments in Business Crime Control in Europe', Ch. 12 in Frances Heidensohn and Martin Farrell (eds.), *Crime In Europe* (1991, Routledge): '.... cartels are in fact a kind of fraud upon competitors and upon the public who are forced to pay more for goods than they would otherwise do' (p. 183).

2 Case 85/76, *Hoffmann-la Roche v Commission* (1979) E.C.R. 461. And see Chapter 2 in this volume.

3 John Temple Lang, 'The Position of Third Parties in EEC Competition Cases', (1978) 3 *European Law Rev.* 177.

4 C. S. Kerse, *EEC Antitrust Procedure* (2nd ed., 1987, European Law Centre).

5 See Cases 32/78 etc, *BMW v Commission* (1979) E.C.R. 2435, p. 2473, and p. 2490 (Advocate General Warner).

6 See generally, Christopher Bellamy and Graham Child, *Common Market Law of Competition* (3rd ed., 1987), p. 545.

7 Case 228/82 etc., *Ford v Commission (No. 2)* (1984) E.C.R. 1129; *BP/TGWU*, Commission's *Sixteenth Report on Competition Policy* (1986), point 43.

8 Case 228/82 etc., *BP/TGWU*, see note 7, above.
9 Case 210/81, *Demo-Studio Schmidt v Commission* (1983) E.C.R. 3045.
10 Ibid., p. 3064.
11 See the summary of national laws in the report prepared for the CCBE (the 'Edwards Report'): D.A.O. Edwards, *The Professional Secret, Confidentiality, and Legal Professional Privilege in the Nine Member States of the European Community* (1975).
12 Cases 209/78 etc., *van Landewyck v Commission* (1980) E.C.R. 3125.
13 Ibid., p. 3239.
14 Ibid., p. 3298.
15 Case 53/85, *AKZO Chemie v Commission* (1986) E.C.R. 1965.
16 Ibid., p. 1992.
17 Ibid.
18 Case 85/76, *Hoffmann-la Roche v Commission* (1979) E.C.R. 471.
19 Ibid., pp. 512–13.
20 Commission, *Twelfth Report on Competition Policy* (1982), point 35.
21 See generally, Neville March Hunnings, 'The Stanley Adams Affair or the Biter Bit', (1987) 24 C.M.L.Rev. 65.
22 Case 85/76, *Hoffmann-la Roche v Commission* (1979) E.C.R. 471.
23 See Hunnings, op. cit., pp. 72–73.
24 Case 145/83, *Adams v Commission* (1985) E.C.R. 3539.
25 Ibid., p. 3587–88.
26 Ibid., pp. 3588–90.
27 Ibid., p. 3540 *et seq*.
28 C. S. Kerse, *EEC Antitrust Procedure* (2nd ed., 1987), p. 209.
29 Commission, *Fifteenth Report on Competition Policy* (1985), point 51.
30 Case 792/79R, *Camera Care v Commission* (1980) E.C.R. 119.
31 Ibid., p. 131.
32 Ibid., pp. 136–7.
33 Ibid., p. 131.
34 *Ford Werke AG*, O.J. 1982, L256/20; *Boosey & Hawkes*, Press Release IP (87) 334, 30.7.87.
35 *ECS/AKZO*, O.J. 1983, L252/13.
36 Commission, *Fifteenth Report on Competition Policy* (1985), point 49.
37 Ibid.
38 Bellamy and Child, op. cit., p. 523.
39 *NCB/National Smokeless Fuels/NCC*, O.J. 1976, L35/6.
40 Case 109/75R, *National Carbonising Co. v Commission* (1975) E.C.R. 1193, p. 1202.
41 See p. 47, of this volume.
42 See pp. 56–7, of this volume.
43 See Case 228/82 etc., *Ford v Commission* (1984) E.C.R. 1129.
44 Cases 43 and 63/82, *VBVB and VBBB v Commission* (1984) 19, 57.
45 Ibid.
46 Cases 142 and 156/84, *BAT and R.J. Reynolds v Commission* (1987) E.C.R. 4487; (1988) 4 C.M.L.R. 24.
47 (1988) 4 C.M.L.R., p. 57.
48 Ibid., p. 56.

49 See, for example, Case 298/83, *CICCE v Commission* (1985) E.C.R 1105.

50 For instance, as in Case 210/81, see note 9 above, and Cases 142 and 156/84, see note 46, above.

51 Case 26/76, *Metro v Commission (No. 1)*, (1977) E.C.R. 1875, p. 1882.

52 Ibid, p. 1899.

53 Ibid., p. 1901.

54 Ibid., p. 1923.

55 Case 264/82, *Timex v Commission* (1985) E.C.R. 849.

56 Case 169/84, *COFAZ v Commission* (1986) E.C.R. 391.

57 Ibid., p. 415.

58 See also Case 191/82, *Fediol v Commission* (1983) E.C.R. 2913 (anti-subsidy proceeding); Case 210/81, see note 9 above (similar situation to that in *Metro*).

59 Cases 142 and 156/84, *BAT and R.J. Reynolds v Commission* (1987), note 46, above.

60 (1988) 4 C.M.L.R., p. 33.

61 Ibid., p. 34.

62 Ibid.

63 Ibid., p. 54.

6 Informal settlement

Given that the Commission's procedure of investigation, hearing and coming to a decision in the field of competition policy is officially conceived as having an administrative character, it is perhaps unsurprising that informal or negotiated settlement should play a prominent role. Indeed, the formal process discussed so far, involving investigation, a statement of objection and full hearing, leading eventually to a formal decision and perhaps imposition of sanctions, is the exception rather than the rule. This results from both constraints on resources and a positive policy of resolving matters where possible by means of a negotiated accommodation rather than formalised prosecution and resort to sanctions. This might suggest then that any analogy with national procedures of criminal law prosecution are in fact largely misplaced and are mainly relevant to a handful of serious, blatant and deliberate infringements. But negotiated settlement, although a matter of low visibility, is an important means of resolution in some areas of national criminal law, especially in relation to offences in the context of economic regulation. Even in the area of 'classical' criminal offending, there is a significant diversion of cases away from the formal process of prosecution and court judgement by means of more or less informal warnings and cautions. In a sense such cautions involve a negotiated settlement: a determination, for instance, that the offence is not especially serious, a concession by the offender that the offence has been committed and an implicit assurance on the part of the latter that the offence will not be repeated. It would be misleading therefore to divorce negotiated settlement from the analogy of criminal proceedings when it is clear that at a national level of criminal procedure issues in relation to prosecution, trial and sentence may be decided in an administrative fashion. Decisions as to prosecution, as to plea and as to sentence may be very much subject to negotiation rather than be resolved by the application of rules in open court. To bring this point into sharper relief, it is proposed first of all in this chapter to say something about settlement procedures at the level of national criminal proceedings.

'Compounding'

'Compounding' is the British term for an out-of-court settlement of a proceeding in relation to certain economic offences, but it is a practice which is common to a number of national systems. Within the U.K., the vast majority of income tax, VAT and customs fraud cases are decided by negotiation rather than by formal prosecution. The Inland Revenue do not have the same statutory powers as the Commissioners of Customs and Excise to enter into 'compounding' but in practice usually arrive at an administrative settlement,[1] whereby full disclosure by the taxpayer is encouraged by the prospect of the Revenue refraining from using criminal proceedings. As Levi states:

> Much of the negotiation in tax cases arises in the context of assessments of how much tax is payable (and how much the Revenue will settle for) rather than in the context of criminal investigation.[2]

The number of Revenue prosecutions stands at a few hundred per year (538 in 1976–77, down to 332 in 1984-85,[3] for example). But in the field of VAT and customs and excise offences, the Customs and Excise have notable statutory powers to settle rather than prosecute. Section 152 of the Customs and Excise Management Act 1979 enables the Customs and Excise to settle with the offender in line with a penalty which would be imposed upon summary conviction; thus in relation to offences under Customs and Excise and VAT legislation, there exists a kind of informal and invisible negotiated penality. Compounding is really some way between a formal penal decision and a purely negotiated settlement. The Customs and Excise must have sufficient evidence to put a case before a criminal court and there is a clear financial penalty; on the other hand, the process is (in practice) confidential, thus avoiding publicity and stigma, and other penalties, in particular imprisonment, are avoided. In principle, there is a kind of 'deal': no prosecution in return for a quickly paid up pecuniary penalty. The policy behind compounding has been explained in a written answer by Treasury Ministers in 1984:[4]

> The decision whether to prosecute or to offer to compound proceedings is taken on the merits of each case. The general factors taken into consideration are the gravity of the offence and the best interests of law enforcement and of the revenue. In view of the pressure on the courts and on departmental resources, it is the Commissioners' policy to offer compounding whenever appropriate. If the offer is refused, they then proceed with the prosecution of the alleged offender.

Passas and Nelken[5] point out that compounding has a number of clear advantages for the Customs and Excise: more money can be recovered; it is faster and cheaper than prosecution; it releases scarce administrative resources; and it focuses the penalty on the real offender, not innocent third parties who may become enmeshed in the impact of a criminal sanction (for instance, employees, who may lose their jobs). Compounding reflects very much a 'value for money' approach and the desire to maximise efficient enforcement. The result is that the process of prosecution is reserved for serious, blatant and recalcitrant cases, which are followed through into the courts for strong retributive or general deterrent reasons. There are some important analogies in this respect with the Commission's approach to competition infringements – again, an agency with scarce manpower resources is concerned to achieve maximum enforcement; but 'value for money' in this context is not so much a question of recouping financial losses brought about by unlawful non-payment, but of minimising economic damage to competition by bringing to an end as quickly as possible undesirable and harmful activities.

Informal settlement, sometimes based upon procedures similar to compounding in the U.K., is also to be found in other national legal systems in relation to offences against economic regulation. Negotiation is an even more significant aspect of this area of criminal law enforcement in the United States.[6] Other European countries display, to varying extents, a willingness to negotiate rather than formally prosecute. In France, in relation to customs and subsidy offences, the policy preference is for an out-of-court settlement,[7] and a settlement may be proposed by either side. If a settlement is not reached, the case will then be passed on to the judicial authorities for formal prosecution. A typical settlement would comprise repayment of the amount of money unlawfully received or withheld, coupled with a small penalty payment.[8] In contrast, German law and practice places much more emphasis on formal prosecution.[9] This may be partly explained by the existence of a legal culture which is relatively speaking very willing to go to court. Even so there is evidence of a certain level of informal settlement,[10] especially if it is felt that an infringement is more of a technicality than a serious or blatant instance of offending.

It is clear enough, therefore, that in the context of economic regulation by means of criminal law, there is a substantial resort to informal negotiated settlement of low visibility at the national level. In addition, reference may be made to other processes of informal settlement, such as plea and charge negotiation and pre-trial review, which operate at different stages of the criminal justice process to produce a negotiated outcome. These processes are well-documented elsewhere and need not be referred to in any detail here, but they serve to emphasise the importance of 'negotiated justice' in the context of national systems of criminal law enforcement.

Settlement of EEC competition cases

The bulk of the Commission's decisions relating to arrangements which may have an anti-competitive character are informal and part of a regular on-going administrative process activated by the parties' voluntary notification of such arrangements. In view of the number of agreements and practices potentially subject to Articles 85 and 86, notification as provided for under Regulation 17 is an administrative necessity, as is the fact that the majority of notified arrangements are dealt with eventually by group exemptions under Article 85(3) or by being approved at a fairly early stage of examination in an informal manner. The Commission's resources allow only a handful of cases to be fully examined and dealt with by means of a formal decision. Table 6.1 presents the statistics from 1987 and illustrates the pattern of the Commission's resolution of its case-load:

Table 6.1 Competition cases dealt with by the Commission by type of resolution procedure in 1987.

Resolution procedure	Number
Formal decisions:	16
– based upon complaint and investigation (one of which was a decision on interim measures)	7
– based upon notification leading to negative clearance or exemption	9
'Procedural' decisions under Articles 11 and 14 of Reg. 17	42
Cases dealt with by 'administrative letter' (mainly arising from notification)	57
Settlement without formal decision because the practices were altered to conform with the competition rules, were terminated or expired	334
– of which, based on notifications of motor vehicle distribution agreements	125

Source: Commission, *Seventeenth Report on Competition Policy* (1987).

Therefore, out of the total of cases finally dealt with (that is, excluding the procedural and interim decisions) only fifteen, or just under 4 per cent, were resolved through a formal decision.The great majority were dealt with by a so-called administrative letter or even less formally with the file being closed. This figure represents the proportion of negotiated settlements for 1987, both as regards notified arrangements and those otherwise brought to the Commission's notice. In practice, whenever the Commission is considering a particular arrangement it is open to informal discussions with the parties concerned; as will be seen later, even in those cases in which a complaint has been made or an investigation carried out, the outcome may be a 'settlement' rather than a formal decision either in favour of or against the 'defending' party.

'Comfort letters'

A certain degree of formality has been introduced into the Commission's settlement procedure with the issue of 'administrative' or 'comfort letters' in some cases. This comprises a written communication to the parties concerned to the effect that the Commission sees no reason to take any further action (good news for the parties, hence 'comfort'). This is in most respects a low visibility settlement: it is rarely published as such, is not a 'decision' of the Commission and therefore almost certainly not subject to review by the Court of Justice, and does not have to be taken on the basis of consultation with other parties, such as the Advisory Committee on Restrictive Practices and Monopolies, or complainants (unless it is a 'formal' comfort letter, discussed further below). The effect of such a letter, then, is to bring to an end the Commission's interest in the matter, on the basis of the facts known to it (it may re-open the file if new or changed facts emerge), although this does not preclude Member State authorities or courts from applying Articles 85(1) or 86 to the arrangement.[11]

Some concern has been expressed as to the lack of transparency in this area[12] and the Commission has adopted the practice in a few cases of issuing a 'formal' comfort letter, which increases the level of visibility in relation to some settlements. In such cases, the Commission will publish a notice in the *Official Journal*, providing essential information about its proposed approval of the practice and inviting third parties to submit any comments within at least one month. Any comfort letter following on from this notice can then be regarded as a 'formal comfort letter' and will be listed in the relevant *Annual Report on Competition Policy*.[13] The Commission has stated that the purpose of this procedure is to 'enhance the declaratory value' of its letter. What is clearly achieved is some opportunity for third parties to be heard, subject to any requirements of confidentiality as would normally apply in Commission hearings. But this procedure is used only in a very small number of cases (for instance three in 1984, one in 1985, one in 1986, none in 1987).

Aspects of negotiation

It is clear therefore that the Commission is often inclined to negotiate rather than prosecute and that much of this negotiation is carried out with little opportunity for outside scrutiny. To what extent does this represent a satisfactory enforcement of competition policy?

An obvious point in favour of negotiation is that, in a context of limited resources, it is a means by which more cases may be dealt with expeditiously and it is in the general interest for alleged or possible infringements of the competition rules to be dealt with and terminated as quickly as possible. Moreover, if the infringements are minor, neither justice nor expediency require a full-scale prosecution. It may also be argued that compliance is better secured by voluntary agreement than through the imposition of stigmatising sanctions; and that the process of negotiation promotes mutual trust and confidence between the Commission and undertakings, which will increase the willingness of the latter to play by the rules. 'Negotiated justice' and 'alternative dispute resolution' have a number of advocates for such reasons, and it is undeniable that the process of formal prosecution and judicial resolution may prove counter-productive, in giving rise to resentment and by polarising attitudes.

In the same way, any doubts which are expressed about settlements in this context reflect the misgivings about negotiated justice more generally, and cluster around the problems of unreviewable discretion, disregard of third party interests and the temptation to place expediency before justice. Some of these misgivings need to be more fully explored.

Since informal settlement between the Commission and defending parties is largely a product of private discussion, suspicions may inevitably be aroused as to whether fair play is guaranteed. In 1982, the European Parliament expressed some concern about the lack of transparency in relation to negotiated competition policy settlements. In its Resolution on the Commission's *Tenth Report on Competition Policy*,[14] it called for more information to be published on the principles and criteria used by the Commission in reaching informal settlements, in order to provide more guidance for undertakings generally. To what extent useful guidance may be obtained from a perusal of the Commission's informal settlement practice is perhaps open to question: the Commission has maintained that its press releases should be confined to cases of real importance, either in terms of legal issues or the market power of the parties involved. But the argument in favour of publication is probably more convincing in relation to the need to guarantee equal treatment. A large body of informal, unpublished decision-making may disguise what is in fact a practice of inconsistent treatment. Van Bael,[15] for instance, argued that the Commission's settlement with Fiat in 1984 was not distinguishable, for the public at large, from its formal decision against British Leyland, which entailed the imposition of a fine. However, this is an argument in favour of wider publication rather than an indication of actual discrimination[16] and both the Commission and major companies will be aware that the terms of any settlement cannot be kept from potential public scrutiny, given the vigilance of consumer organisations and MEPs. The context of informal settlement is very different at the European level; unlike national criminal proceedings, there are likely to be a number of interested parties, such as competitors or consumer bodies, who will have the necessary awareness and incentive to probe the outcome.

Undue influence is another matter of concern. The private nature of negotiation with the Commission may allow lobbying to take place which could influence the Commission's response, and so lead to distributive injustice. The question of lobbying on behalf of certain defendant undertakings was raised squarely in the European Parliament in 1984[17] and the Commission's answer was sanguine as to the acceptability of 'representations' made on behalf of companies involved in competition proceedings. In its view, such parties:

> are at liberty to decide who will act on their behalf and the Commission is not required within the framework of the procedure established by Regulation 17/62 to question the reasons why a particular representative is acting in a given case.[18]

The Commission clearly wishes to maintain the maximum level of flexibility in its procedure and rely upon the rights of appeal of parties with a 'legitimate interest' against either formal decisions or refusal to take the proceedings any further (see the discussion in the previous chapter) as a means of ensuring and demonstrating fair play. However, there remains a certain level of scepticism; Van Bael asks why proceedings are taken more frequently against companies from some Member States than from others or why non-EEC firms tend to attract larger fines. But it would be rash to impute such patterns to governmental lobbying or political influence. Other explanations, in particular the location of larger and/or more anti-competitive companies in certain States, need to be tested first of all (see in this respect the analysis of activity which has been subject to formal Commission proceedings in Chapter 8).

The Court of Justice has been supportive of the Commission being able to exercise a discretion to reach a settlement rather than pursue a case all the way through its procedure. In a judgement in 1984[19] the Court stressed that the Commission's procedure 'presents an opportunity for the undertakings concerned to adapt the practices at issue to the rules of the Treaty'.[20] The Court repeated this argument in *BAT and Reynolds*[21] and added that for the possibility of such compliance to be real:

> the companies and the Commission must be entitled to enter into confidential negotiations in order to determine what alterations will remove the cause for the Commission's objections .... Such a right would be imperilled if the complainants were to attend the negotiations or be kept informed of the progress made in order to submit their observations on the proposals put forward by one party or the other.[22]

During the same case it was also suggested that the Commission had been subject to political pressure in the course of the negotiations, but the Court could not consider this argument in view of the lack of evidence in support of the allegation.[23] The overall tenor of the Court's judgement remained very sympathetic to the need for negotiated settlements.

Negotiation of sanctions: 'plea bargaining'

Another possible area of negotiation relates to the eventual adoption of a formal decision and in particular the nature and extent of any sanction which may be imposed as part of such a decision. The analogy which suggests itself here is the familiar practice of charge and plea bargaining in criminal proceedings at a national level; a lesser sanction may be promised in return for the defending party agreeing to plead guilty, provide evidence, or otherwise help the pursuit of justice. Both prosecuting authorities and court administrators may benefit from such a practice, in that it relieves workload and so saves time and cost. But this form of negotiation is controversial at the national level, since it necessarily involves a compromise of rights of defence in return for a lesser sanction: there is the equal possibility that the innocent may be pressed into conceding guilt and that the guilty gain an undue advantage simply by conceding rights, the exercise of which may not have helped them in any case. In so far as such negotiation is invisible and unregulated it will continue to give rise to concern on both these scores. Yet the familiar dilemma reappears – if the negotiation is opened up to outside scrutiny in order to ensure fair play to everybody, it may then become more inhibited and less effective.[24]

Not surprisingly, there is no formal provision for this kind of negotiation in proceedings involving the Commission. However, there have been cases in which sanctions have been mitigated following a waiver of procedural rights or the giving of an undertaking as to future conduct. When dealing with the *Zinc Producers' Cartel* in 1984[25] the Commission openly took into account as a mitigating circumstance the fact that 'all the undertakings concerned cooperated in clearing up the affair after the sending of the statement of objections', in determining the amount of the fine.[26] Cooperation during the proceedings was similarly taken into account when dealing with the *Woodpulp Cartel*.[27] There, an undertaking as to future conduct was held by the Commission to justify a substantial reduction in the normal level of fines for such a case, since the undertaking by the cartel members was,[28] in the Commission's view, likely to improve conditions of competition in that market and so lessen the risk of future infringements. Such an outcome would therefore contribute to the Commission's future task of monitoring conditions of competition and could also be seen as a form of prospective cooperation. In such decisions the Commission appears to have modified its earlier attitude expressed in the *Michelin* case,[29] to the effect that cooperation was no ground for reducing the amount of a fine, since the parties were under a basic duty to cooperate during the administrative procedure in any case. Advocate General Verloren van Themaat was of the same view[30] and added that during the procedure the Commission ought not to give any indication of the likely amount of a fine, since this can only be properly determined when the procedure is completed. But it is clear that a strict application of that legalistic principle would undermine any frank exchange between the Commission and the defending parties aimed at encouraging the latter's cooperation. The Commission's more recent approach suggests that it is willing to go some way towards compromising rigorous enforcement, if clear future advantages are in its view a strong possibility.

Willingness on the part of defending parties to take remedial action may certainly be viewed favourably by the Commission in deciding on the *kind* of sanction. In its *National Panasonic* decision in 1982 the Commission took into account the 'constructive attitude' of the Japanese parent company Matsushita in establishing an antitrust compliance programme in consultation with the Commission.[31] This involved an audit of legal practice and the issuing of codes of conduct to subsidiaries. This comes close to a sentencing discount based upon expressions of remorse and indications of rehabilitation, a process once again familiar in national criminal proceedings. Similar action had been taken by General Motors in 1975, when that company acted immediately to reduce the level of its charges and reimburse customers excess amounts which had been collected,[32] and so earned a reduction in its fine. Voluntary termination of an infringement prior to the Commission even reaching its decision – a form of prompt confession and making amends – may also prove a successful strategy in mitigation, reducing the amount of a fine, as United Brands discovered in 1976,[33] or may even prompt the Commission to close the file.[34] In some cases, companies have given undertakings about future market behaviour, with similar results, as in the instance of the *Woodpulp Cartel*, noted above.

Negotiated settlement and the idea of 'administrative proceedings'

Reliance on an informal, negotiated resolution of breaches of the competition rules is clearly an important feature of the Commission's approach to enforcement in this area. Much of the debate to date relates not so much to its efficacy as to its transparency and the need to subject this kind of process to legal scrutiny. Any need for legal control is related to more general arguments concerning the nature of the Commission's proceedings and how far the analogy with a national criminal procedure can be taken. This analogy is at its strongest when discussing the formal process of investigation, hearings and sanctions as laid down in Regulations 17 and 99. In that context, as has been seen, procedural guarantees have been evolved which draw their inspiration largely from the model of criminal procedure. However, when the Commission is minded to negotiate a settlement, informality and flexibility come to the fore, and the Court of Justice has been supportive of the Commission in playing down the 'adversary' element in its procedure, especially in its judgement in *BAT and Reynolds*.[35] But it is doubtful whether classification of a proceeding as 'adversary' or 'administrative' really helps in this debate, since in national criminal proceedings the same problem arises as to how far informal settlement should be allowed to take place and in effect supplant the formal adversary procedures which are laid down by law. The real issue, then, is rather to identify the advantages of an informal negotiated settlement and to determine to what extent it should be used in place of more visible formal proceedings.

The advantages of informal settlement have been referred to already and may be summarised in terms of cost-effectiveness and the speedy termination of unlawful situations. Against this must be weighed the importance of a full and formal prosecution, with its associated features of high visibility, legal rigour and demands on resources. In relation to competition infringements there may be said to be a number of factors which tip the balance in some cases in favour of informal settlement. The first is the level of ambiguity in moral condemnation: such breaches are not treated as criminal offences under all national systems. This variable position may be seen at a glance: criminal under U.S. law, not at all criminal in the U.K., and 'administrative' offences under German law. The second is the lack of sharp legal definition in relation to many such infringements. Abuse of a dominant position under Article 86 is a good example – it may not be very easy for companies to predict in advance whether their conduct will be assessed as abusive in this sense. And thirdly, the economic context of anti-competitive behaviour is often complex (for instance, the formation of 'crisis cartels'), and this may render the use of formal, legalistic procedures and sanctions a blunt instrument of control which fails to address sufficiently the underlying structural causes of the breach of the rules. Even if it is accepted that anti-competitive behaviour is a form of delinquency, it can be argued in many instances to be of a different order from much 'traditional' criminal offending and that, perhaps most persuasively, its control (as with many other examples of 'economic' offending) is best managed through informal procedures of negotiation and persuasion, with only the most blatant cases being reserved for formal prosecution. It is on the basis of such argument that resort to informal settlement should be justified, rather than by simply asserting descriptions of the process as 'administrative' or 'non-adversary', which only serves to beg further questions about the adoption of such procedures.

Notes

1 See Michael Levi, *Regulating Fraud: White Collar Crime and the Criminal Process* (1987, Tavistock), pp. 183–186.
2 Ibid., p. 185.
3 Ibid., p. 186.
4 Hansard, House of Commons, col. 542, 25 April 1984.
5 Nikos Passas and David Nelken, 'The Legal Responses to Agricultural Fraud in the European Community' (unpublished paper, 1991).
6 S. Shapiro, *Wayward Capitalists* (1983, Yale University Press); M. Galanter, 'Judicial Mediation in the United States', 12 (1985) *Journal of Law and Society* 1.
7 M. Delmas-Marty and E. Roche-Pire, *Marché Commun et Criminalité des Affaires* (1982, Economica).
8 Passas and Nelken, op. cit.
9 Ibid.
10 Ibid.

11 Cases 253/78 etc, *Procureur de la République v Giry and Guerlain* (1980) E.C.R. 2327.

12 Ivo Van Bael, 'Comment on the EEC Commission's Antitrust Settlement Practice', 22 (1984) *Swiss Review of International Competition Law* 67.

13 See the Commission's Notice on this procedure, O.J. 1983, C295/6.

14 O.J. 1982, C11/78.

15 Ivo Van Bael, op. cit., p. 68.

16 Compare the details of the two cases: *Fiat*, Commission's *Fourteenth Report on Competition Policy* p. 65; *British Leyland*, O.J. 1984, L207/11.

17 O.J. 1984, C225/20.

18 Ibid.

19 Cases 43 and 63/82, *VBVB and VBBB v Commission* (1984) E.C.R. 19.

20 Ibid., p. 68.

21 Cases 142 and 156/84, *BAT and R.J. Reynolds v Commission* (1987) E.C.R. 4487; (1988) 4 C.M.L.R. 24, at p. 57.

22 Ibid., p. 57.

23 Ibid.

24 See, for instance the research by Baldwin into pre-trial discussions in magistrates' courts in Leeds and Nottingham – the more formal discussions in open court in Leeds were more inhibited and judged less effective: J. R. Baldwin, 'Pre-Trial Settlement in Magistrates' Courts', (1985) 24 *Howard Journal of Criminal Justice* 108.

25 O.J. 1984, L220/27.

26 Ibid., p. 44.

27 O.J. 1985, L85/1, at p. 26. See also Case 226/84, *British Leyland v Commission* (1986) E.C.R. 3263.

28 See O.J. 1985, L85/50-51.

29 Case 322/81, *Michelin v Commission* (1983) E.C.R. 3461, p. 3493.

30 Ibid., p. 3546.

31 O.J. 1982, L354/28.

32 *General Motors*, O.J. 1975, L29/14.

33 *United Brands*, O.J. 1976, L95/1.

34 *Unilever and H. Leverton* (1985), Commission's *Fifteenth Report on Competition Policy*, p. 63 (point 57).

35 See cases referred to in note 21, above.

7 Sanctions

Termination of infringements

It is a logical consequence of the Commission's power to decide that certain practices are in breach of the competition rules that such a decision should include any necessary order to give effect to the decision. Article 3(1) of Regulation 17 explicitly provides that the Commission may require the parties concerned to bring the infringement to an end. What is necessary for this purpose will clearly depend on the nature of the infringement: a negative 'cease and desist order' may suffice, or it may be necessary to require the parties to take positive action (for instance, to change a pricing policy, or supply a customer). In practice, the distinction between a 'positive' and a 'negative' order may not be either meaningful or significant. What is important to note is that the Court of Justice has largely confirmed the Commission's requirement for a range of powers in this respect.

'Cease and desist' orders, provided that they identify the activity which must be stopped with sufficient precision,[1] are unlikely to prove problematical. Immediate compliance may prove difficult in some cases and a period of grace may therefore be allowed (as in the case of *British Telecommunications* in 1982, in respect of its arrangements for message forwarding – a period of two months was granted).[2] A cease and desist order may be given prospective teeth by specifically banning similar conduct in the future. The Swedish manufacturer of cameras, Hasselblad, was prohibited from repeating any of the distribution arrangements condemned by the Commission in 1981.[3]

A requirement for positive action may prove more controversial, however, but there is no doubt that Article 3(1) encompasses this kind of order. The point was argued before the Court of Justice by the American chemicals company Commercial Solvents when it challenged the Commission's decision to the effect that its refusal to supply a competitor with crucial raw materials amounted to a breach of Article 86. Commercial Solvents and its Italian subsidiary contested the Commission's order to supply the other company with a certain quantity of the chemical within a given time at a maximum price. The Court confirmed that the Commission had the power to require such action 'to ensure that its decision was effective'.[4] Advocate General Warner pointed out that there was nothing unusual in such a power, which is found under Member State law (for instance, Article 24 of the Netherlands Economic Competition Law); and also that it was presumed by the logic of Article 3, which in its third paragraph enabled the Commission to make recommendations for the termination of infringements. As to the generality of the wording used in Article 3(1), he argued that this was inevitable owing to the variety of forms that infringements could take: it would have proven impossible to provide a catalogue of measures capable of being ordered by the Commission.[5] The order made in relation to Commercial Solvents is also illustrative of the remedial and preventive aspects of such measures, as distinct from the punitive character of fines. The Commission not only ordered specific supplies to be made but also required the submission of proposals as to longer-term supplies. This was therefore in the nature of a 'life-line' measure, concerned to ensure the commercial survival of a competitor whose viability was at risk. This indicates the essence of the sanction embodied in Article 3; the exercise of the Commission's powers under that provision is more a matter of ensuring competition and thus has a *constructive* character, and is not so much concerned with the allocation of responsibity in a retributive manner, which is province of Article 15 of the Regulation.

Over time, the Commission has ordered a range of measures in exercising its powers under Article 3(1): reporting back (for example, *United Brands*);[6] supplying products (for example, *Commercial Solvents*); review of pricing policy (for example, *ECS/AKZO*[7] – in *United Brands*, Advocate General Mayras commented: 'The Commission is fully entitled ... to require an undertaking ... to abide by a specific price bracket or, if you prefer it, to act as a prices "Commissioner");[8] and divestiture of a company (*Continental Can*).[9] In *Continental Can* the defendant company was required to divest itself of another company which it had acquired contrary, in the view of the Commission, to Article 86 of the Treaty. This order never took effect, however, since the Commission's decision was overruled by the Court of Justice on its merits. For the most part, orders for divestiture following mergers, takeovers or the setting up of joint ventures remain an untested option. Such divestiture was informally agreed in *Automobile Safety Glass*,[10] when the parties to a joint venture agreed to the divestiture of joint interests under the supervision of the Commission. What these cases concerning supplies, pricing and corporate structure illustrate is the potential for constructive and even long-term monitoring of a particular situation in order to guarantee a sufficient level of competition.

It is therefore necessary to emphasise that the outcome of decision-making under Article 3(1) may be much more complex than the conventional idea of 'cease and desist'. Such prohibitory orders, like penalties, suggest finality and a closing of the file. But both the Commission and the Court have been prepared to consider the employment of longer-term measures of supervision and reporting back, especially in relation to infringements of Article 86. The relevant sanctioning concept in this respect is thus one of 'administrative control', not so much penality, although the two approaches may be used in tandem.

Fines

In contrast to the remedial functions of the Commission's powers under Article 3 of Regulation 17, the power to impose fines under Article 15 is clearly penal in nature and should be seen as a response to breaches as a form of delinquency rather than to infringements as a disturbance of competition. The repressive machinery of Article 15 is reserved for those undertakings who are in a position to judge the consequences of their conduct in terms of competition policy and who deliberately or carelessly flout established rules. For this reason, the Commission did not resort to its power to impose penalties until the content of its competition policy had become sufficiently worked out to enable market participants to predict the legal consequences of their behaviour. As in the case of full investigations and formal hearings, fines will in practice be imposed in a relatively small number of cases representing significant and blatant violations.

The power to impose fines once more suggests the model of criminal proceedings. Although not formally of a criminal law character, the fines which may be imposed under Article 15 are designed and employed as punitive and deterrent measures; the formal label cannot disguise their repressive role and indeed the law and practice which has been developed by the Commission and the Court of Justice is highly reminiscent of what would be described as a sentencing policy under a national system. As Advocate General Mayras remarked:

> Although in the strict sense of the term the fines prescribed by Article 17 are not in the nature of criminal-law sanctions, I do not consider it possible, in interpreting the term 'intentionally', to disregard the concepts which are commonly accepted in the penal legislation of the Member States.[11]

But in contrast to the potential variety of measures which may be adopted under Article 3(1), the Commission's repertoire of punitive sanctions is limited to this one pecuniary measure. This is different from the position in some national systems which categorise competition infringements as criminal offences: so, for instance, punitive damages may be awarded under United States law, under which sentences of imprisonment are also possible (although rarely used in practice);[12] under French law establishments may be closed down; under Belgian and Norweigan law a person or undertaking may be excluded from business activities; and under Japanese law a company official may be obliged to resign. Penalties under the Community system therefore appear at first sight to be relatively straightforward, although it will be seen that the fining mechanism may be tuned to reflect the character and gravity of the infringement.

The punitive and deterrent character of these fines was confirmed by the Court of Justice in its *Pioneer* judgement in 1980.[13] The Court stated that the Commission's task:

> certainly includes the duty to investigate and punish individual infringements

and that, in deciding on the amount of a fine, the Commission should:

> ensure that its action has the necessary deterrent effect, especially as regards those types of infringement which are particularly harmful to the attainment of the objectives of the Community.[14]

Advocate General Slynn also stressed the deterrent function of fines in his opinion in that case.[15] There can be little doubt, therefore, as to the purpose of the measures under Article 15 and the constitutional sensitivity of some Member States which requires these penalties to be of a 'non-criminal law character' cannot disguise the essential fact that they are a response to offending conduct and that the relevant concepts in this discussion are thus 'offence' and 'punishment'.

While it is easy enough to identify the penalty, specifying the offence in this context is less straightforward. Leaving to one side for the present fines which are imposed for procedural infringements, such as failure to provide information or the supply of wrong information, under Article 15(1), the fine for the substantive 'offence' is laid down in Article 15(2) quite simply as being in respect of an intentional or negligent breach of Articles 85(1) or 86 of any condition laid down under Article 85(3) in the grant of an exemption. One way to view this would be to say that any intentional or negligent breach of the competition rules is in principle an 'offence' since it is potentially subject to a fine. The problem with such a broad interpretation is that it corresponds neither with practice (the majority of such infringements do not attract fines) nor with the legal evaluation of the Commission and the Court of Justice. Article 15(2) also states that the amount of the fine should be decided with regard to the gravity and duration of the infringement. In fact, such factors do very much determine whether or not a fine will be imposed and it is now clear from the practice of the Commission that both the market behaviour of undertakings and the impact of anti-competitive practices are important components of the 'offence'. In practice, then, there is a distinction between infringements generally and those which have an especially offensive character (and so may be described as 'offences') and for that reason are likely to attract fines. Moreover, the definition of 'offending' (that is, punishable) conduct is largely worked out by using the criteria for imposing fines. In a sense, the offence is identified by working backwards from the decision whether or not to impose a penalty. On the face of it, this process involves circular reasoning: when is a breach of the competition rules an 'offence'? When it is punishable. When is it punishable? When it is sufficiently offensive to deserve punishment. But this is not an unknown process in the evolution of criminal liability, especially when such liability is a matter of degree (for instance, as in the case of manslaughter on the basis of gross negligence, under English criminal law). What has happened in the context of Article 15(2) is that the Commission has used its discretion to impose fines as an instrument for evolving the criteria of liability to be fined. The text of Article 15 has furnished some very broad guidelines in this respect (an intentional or negligent state of mind; the seriousness of the breach), but for the most part the idea of an 'offence' or punishable breach has been worked out by the Commission and the Court of Justice in a body of case-law concerning the imposition of fines.

'Punishable' infringements

Looking at this body of decisions over the last twenty years or more it is possible to identify a number of constituent elements of this substantive anti-competitive offence. There is clearly a mental element of awareness arising from the terms 'intentional' and 'negligent'. But the infringement itself must satisfy certain criteria of seriousness, judged mainly from the surrounding behaviour of the parties concerned and the impact of, or harm caused by, the anti-competitive practice. Broadly, what is impugned under Article 15(2) is a blatant and significant infringement which displays a conscious disregard of the rules and which substantially damages competition.

Intentional or negligent conduct

This element conveys the moral condemnation of the behaviour which justifies a penal response. The parties knew, or ought to have known, that they were acting contrary to the established rules and nonetheless went on to commit a breach. In terms of moral opprobrium, intentional breaches are clearly more serious than those perpetrated through carelessness and the amount of a fine can reflect this difference. However, the Commission's decisions do not always clearly distinguish on the facts between deliberate and negligent action, which may not be surprising in view of evidential problems; resort to a formula of 'at least negligent, if not intentional' is therefore understandable. The Commission used this 'play safe' formula for instance in the *Pioneer* case,[16] even though the Court subsequently held that the infringements were intentional: 'Pioneer must have been fully aware that its conduct was of such a nature as to encourage restrictions', which was sufficient for purposes of intentionality.[17] A general awareness is therefore sufficient to attract liability; the degree of deliberation becomes relevant only as to whether the conduct comprises the 'greater' or 'lesser' version of the offence, which in turn is mainly relevant to the amount of the fine.

On the whole, 'intention' in this context would seem to connote a clear awareness of and willingness to bring about an anti-competitive state of affairs. It is not necessary to show that the parties were clearly aware of the Community rules which were being breached. In the *Miller Schallplatten* case,[18] the Court considered that it was of little relevance to establish that the applicant knew that it was infringing the prohibition of Article 85. In practice, an awareness that competition is being restricted would be sufficient. In the *Pioneer* case, the Pioneer Company organised a meeting at which action against parallel imports was discussed; such an act by a company involved in international sales would be enough to impute intention and, in the view of Advocate General Slynn, any ignorance of the law does not excuse the behaviour or render the infringement negligent.[19] Similarly, to sign an agreement in the full knowledge that its effect would be to make parallel imports more difficult, if not impossible, would amount to a deliberate anti-competitive act, irrespective of actual knowledge of Article 85(1).[20] On the other hand, the alleged infringement of Article 86 by General Motors in 1973 was found by the Court to be a restrictive act carried out inadvertently and quickly remedied, and the Commission's decision imposing a fine for intentional infringement was overruled.[21] Advocate General Mayras argued that the company's policy 'had not been established intentionally in order to distort competition and knowingly to handicap those imports ....'[22]

An intention to restrict competition may be corroborated by evidence that the parties had been advised that their action did or would infringe the competition rules. Indeed, in such cases there may be an additional 'intention to flout' which may aggravate the offending conduct. In the *BMW* case,[23] the company sought legal advice on its circulars and that advice was that they were contrary to Article 85(1) but that with certain amendments their incompatibility would not be 'too flagrant'.[24] The fact that the company proceeded to issue the circulars clearly demonstrated its anti-competitive intent. In such cases, this intention is necessarily deduced from surrounding circumstances, which point to an awareness of the restrictive character of the acts in question. Covert behaviour may be damning in such a context. The members of the Quinine Cartel[25] discussed the advantages and disadvantages of notifying their activities to the Commission and, having decided not to do so, took great efforts to keep their activities secret. Thus a range of evidence may be used to establish knowledge and awareness of anti-competitive behaviour and an intention to behave in such a way may well be deduced from this kind of evidence.

In any case – and especially as legal doctrine becomes more well established and widely disseminated – companies operating at a European or international level are expected to have an 'antitrust awareness'; there is almost an implication that such firms would be acting irresponsibly if they did not inform themselves of the requirements of competition law. Thus the Dutch Michelin company (NBIM) was regarded by the Commission as:

> part of a concern occupying a position on the European market such that it may be expected of the undertaking that it will follow developments in European law attentively and gear its policy to them.[26]

Antitrust awareness is not really problematical in the context of 'classic' infringements, such as export bans and collusive activities in relation to prices and quotas – these are now well established as offending conduct, but in some contexts, such as that of abuse of a dominant position under Article 86, the arguments are less clear-cut. For instance, Hoffmann-la Roche argued in 1979 that the content of Article 86 was still insufficiently precise for purposes of identifying the degree of wrongful behaviour which would justify the imposition of a fine.[27] It based this argument on well established principles such as legal certainty and *nullum crimen sine lege*, urging that there should be no punishment if the concepts upon which the sanction is based and their interpretation are open to argument. The Commission's response to this point, which was accepted by the Court, stressed both the inevitable generality in the drafting of competition 'offences' and the need for antitrust awareness on the part of large companies:

> Competition law must, to be effective, take into account multiple aspects of economic life and cannot avoid references to general concepts 'requiring to a large extent interpretation by the Court' and ... concepts were well known to undertakings which, like the applicant, engage in international commerce and are familiar with national competition legislation.[28]

In its judgement, the Court referred to the responsibilities of a 'vigilant commercial operator'[29] and doubted whether in fact Roche could not have been aware of either its market dominance or the anti-competitive character of its system of fidelity rebates. In the view of the Court, the company's internal documents established that it had intentionally pursued 'a commercial policy designed to bar the access to the market of new competitors' and its market share suggested that its claimed innocence as to awareness of market dominance could only be the outcome of an inadequate study of market structures or a refusal to take such circumstances into consideration.[30] In other words, large and experienced companies will not be allowed (perhaps cynically) to plead naïvety or ignorance; at that level, ignorance of law is no defence and antitrust awareness is expected. Smaller traders may be viewed more leniently, however. In its decision concerning the 'Toltec' and 'Dorcet' trade marks,[31] the Commission imposed a fine on the Dutch BAT subsidiary, but not on the small trader Segers, 'the owner of a small Dutch firm, who at the beginning of his dispute with BAT was not adequately informed about the German legal position and Community law'.

Similar considerations apply to the concept of a negligent infringement. Even if there is no evidence that undertakings deliberately set out to obtain an anti-competitive advantage, as time goes on most companies will be held to be in a position where they *should* have been aware of the unacceptably restrictive nature of their behaviour. Much will depend on the degree to which the illegality of the conduct in question is clearly established and it is not surprising to find some earlier cases in which uncertainty in this respect militated against the use of fines. In its decision in *Vegetable Parchments* in 1978, the Commission refrained from imposing a fine, since at the time in question the rules of competition relating to exchanges of information had not been sufficiently developed.[32] It should also be borne in mind that certain situations will preclude any penalty – notification of an arrangement under Article 17, a 'comfort letter' from the Commission, being covered by a group exemption – and a *bona fide* and reasonable reliance on such situations, even if mistaken, could well stop the imposition of a fine. For instance, a wrong, but not unreasonable belief that they were covered by the group exemption under Regulation 67 saved the parties in *BP Kemi-DDSF* from a fine.[33]

Awareness of anti-competitive behaviour, or its probability, is not defeated by the argument that a party was forced into that activity. Nevertheless, such pressure may be taken into account as a mitigating factor and fines may be reduced or waived altogether, depending on the circumstances. In a number of cases involving distribution agreements, dealers who have been effectively forced into committing infringements have been treated leniently on that account. In the *Hasselblad* case in 1982, for instance, the dealers supplied by the Swedish company only reluctantly agreed to cooperate in its policy of partitioning the market and this was taken into account in fixing the amount of the fine.[34]

Behaviour of the parties

To some extent the parties' behaviour may be judged by the mental element of deliberation or carelessness. But there are also other circumstances which may be relevant in assessing any delinquency in this context. In particular, infringement of the competition rules which is persistent, contumacious or covert will render the 'offence' more serious as will the taking of a leading or directing role in a cartel or other restrictive practice. The former aspects of behaviour were present in the infringement established by the Commission in 1984 on the part of the *Benelux Flat Glass Cartel*.[35] Two members of the cartel, St. Gobain and BSN, had been found guilty of infringing Article 85 on three previous occasions and both companies had established undercover relationships in contravention of an agreement previously entered into with the Commission, which provided for a severing of their earlier links. The recidivism and covert defiance of the Commission were considered to be aggravating factors which justified heavy fines. Similarly, the 'institutionalised' collusion of the members of the *Polypropylene Cartel*, following earlier unsuccessful 'crisis cartel' discussions with the Commission, was viewed seriously.[36] Some of the undertakings involved in this cartel, such as Hoechst, ICI and BASF, had already been the subjects of fines imposed for collusion in the chemicals industry, when the *Dyestuffs (Aniline Dyes) Cartel* had been dealt with in 1969.[37] The Commission also singled out the ringleaders of the Polypropylene Cartel for heavier fines, since the four largest producers (Montepolimeri, ICI, Hoechst and Shell):

> formed the nucleus of the arrangements and constituted an unofficial directorate the members of which considered themselves to have a special responsibility towards ensuring the success of the cartel.[38]

All of these factors contribute to a profile of proven determination and initiative in flouting the competition rules and provide the touchstone of antitrust delinquency.

On the other hand, even the most serious offenders may redeem their position to some extent by adopting an accommodating and cooperative attitude once their infringement has been established. The way in which a helpful and compliant attitude may have an effect on sanctions or lead to a negotiated outcome has already been discussed in the previous chapter. However, it is open to argument to what extent a highly delinquent company should be able to benefit from what might be a calculated change of heart once the game is up. In its *Polypropylene* decision, the Commission conceded a little in the way of mitigation for co-operation in so far as account was taken that:

> a very few of the producers cooperated (but not to the extent that they claim) with the Commission's investigations, at least once the incriminating evidence had been discovered.[39]

Harm caused by the anti-competitive practice

Article 85(1) refers to activities having either an anti-competitive object or effect. It is therefore possible in principle to penalise undertakings for conceiving an anti-competitive act without putting it into effect or its causing any actual harm. Atochem, a member of the *Polypropylene Cartel*, argued that it had (itself) cheated on its fellow cartel members and was competing during the operation of the cartel; but in the view of the Court of First Instance, that was no ground for mitigating its fine since it had actively assisted in the setting up of the cartel.[40] But in the majority of cases, the impact of anti-competitive activity on the market is an important component of punishable behaviour under Article 15. This is in the nature of the system of control; rarely is the Commission in a position to surprise a restrictive practice which is about to be implemented – normally it will be responding to past or continuing events and so is well able to consider the effects in assessing gravity.

The concept of market impact itself has a number of elements. What is at issue here is the totality of the harm done to conditions of competition on a particular market. The extent of the harm can be measured by reference to the market share of the parties and their annual turnover, since these elements in turn point to the number of persons who may be adversely affected, as competitors, traders or consumers, and to the level of undue profit gained from an unlawful practice. Similarly, the duration of the practice will serve as a guide to these matters. And then the 'depth' of the anti-competitive practice, in the sense of restriction of commercial opportunities and access to a market, may be taken into account. Thus an efficient system of preventing parallel imports, which effectively eliminates competition, has greater 'depth' and gravity compared to, for instance, some form of cooperation between competitors which restricts competition as to only some aspects of their commercial activity (such as research and development, for example). A brief glance at the fines imposed so far reveals that there are a few major categories of activity which have attracted penalties, notably export bans, price fixing, market sharing and abuse of a dominant position (in other words, 'classic' infringements). There is therefore a good deal of regularity and predictability as regards the kind of restrictive practice which will be subject to fines, and this reinforces the arguments of the Commission and the Court in relation to 'antitrust awareness'. The other elements of market impact referred to above, such as market share, turnover, profit, duration and loss caused to others are likely to be more relevant to the *amount* of a fine, rather than the issue of whether a fine should be imposed.

Scaling the fines

As with the case of criminal law fines, some guidance in terms of minimum and maximum limits is provided in Article 15: fines for substantive infringements under Article 15(2) may be imposed within a range extending between the minimum of one thousand ECU (originally units of account) and the alternative maxima of a million ECU or 10 per cent of the parties' turnover in the preceding business year. The turnover maximum may give rise to complex calculations and result in fines of a considerable amount – as much as 75 million ECU in the recent case of Tetra Pak, the Swiss manufacturer of liquid packaging, for a deliberate policy of aiming to eliminate competitors, contrary to Article 86.[41] The purpose of the turnover maximum is to relate the quantum of larger fines to the parties' ability to pay and to achieve an appropriate level of punishment, both in retributive and deterrent terms – anything less than a million ECU may not have sufficient impact upon larger multinational companies.

An important issue in practice is whether turnover should be interpreted to mean turnover in all goods throughout the world or more narrowly as that in the goods affected by the infringement. This point was debated in the *Pioneer* case[42] where the parties fined argued against the use of global turnover for this purpose. The Court of Justice pointed out, however, that nothing in the wording of Article 15(2) suggested that a global turnover (that is, all goods throughout the world) should not be used as the maximum penalty. As Advocate General Slynn argued, the narrower interpretation would mean that:

> where a very large conglomerate with diversified interests engages in a very serious infringement of Community law in one of the sectors in which it is engaged, the Commission would lack the power to impose a fine of sufficient size to amount to a real deterrent.[43]

On the other hand, both the Court and the Advocate General considered that *some* account should be taken of diversification, especially if an infringement is committed in only a small sector of a company's interests, since in that case the delinquency is not spread throughout its activities. The principle which emerges then places global turnover at the top of the range, but allows turnover in the goods concerned in the infringement to be taken into account when appropriate. In the words of the Court:

> ... it is permissible ... to have regard both to the total turnover of the undertaking, which gives an indication, albeit approximate and imperfect, of the size of the undertaking and of its economic power, and to the proportion of that turnover accounted for by the goods in respect of which the infringement was committed, which gives an indication of the scale of the infringement.[44]

But neither turnover figure should be allowed by itself to dictate simplistically the amount of the fine. The application of this principle is illustrated by the *Pioneer* case itself. For instance, the German company Melchers, one of the defending parties (all European distributors of the Japanese 'Pioneer' hi-fi equipment), had argued that, since only 10 per cent of its turnover related to hi-fi products, that fact should justify a reduction in its fine. The Court of Justice appeared to accept that argument in itself, but also to offset against such mitigation the fact that:

> Melchers, as a result of the diversity of its activities, of which the sale of Pioneer products constituted only a small part, could more easily have resisted the pressure exerted upon it [by the distributors' cartel].[45]

It therefore appears that calculation of turnover in the first place involves a choice between a maximum scale based on global turnover and a possibly lower scale based on turnover in products and in a geographical area relevant to the infringement; and secondly the location of the fine as a percentage of the turnover will depend upon other relevant factors such as that just referred to in Melchers' case. Fixing a fine at the top end of the scale (by using global turnover) would usually reflect a very serious violation and perhaps an element of exemplary punishment. So, for instance, when dealing with the *Benelux Flat Glass Cartel*,[46] the Commission assessed the fines on the 'recidivist' cartel members BSN and St. Gobain by reference to flat glass turnover in other countries as well as Benelux, whereas the other parties' fines were based on their Benelux turnover alone. The process of fine assessment on the basis of turnover is depicted in Table 7.1.

Table 7.1 The process of fine assessment

Scale 1	Scale 2
(global turnover)	(turnover in products and in the area relating to the infringement)
——————— 100% e.g. ——————— 100,000,000 ECU	——————— 100% e.g. ——————— 10,000,000 ECU
10% (10,000,000 ECU)	10% (1,000,000 ECU)

fine adjusted according to
factors such as duration, role in
cartel, 'antitrust awareness',
impact on other parties etc.

In some cases the difference between the global turnover and that relevant to the area of the infringement may be considerable. In *Pioneer*, for example, the fine ultimately imposed on Pioneer Europe was two million units of account, which represented about 2 per cent of its total turnover, but 10 per cent of its turnover in hi-fi products in France, Germany and the U.K. in 1976.[47] Therefore, if the base for calculation was turnover in hi-fi equipment in those three countries, the fine would have been the maximum possible and obviously substantial. But the Court had reduced the original fine imposed by the Commission from 3.5 million units of account since there had been insufficient evidence for the existence of the restrictive practice throughout all of the period alleged by the Commission. This implies that the Court was assessing the fine on the basis of global turnover, since otherwise it would be maintaining it at a maximum level. But the Court's own words in its *Pioneer* judgement should be kept in mind: that fixing an appropriate fine cannot be the result of a simple calculation based on turnover.

The impact of fines

Since the fines are intended to embody both an appropriate quantum of punishment in retributive terms and a sufficient deterrent impact, some account may need to be taken of the actual effect of the sanctions on those companies subject to the fines. In particular, if any attempt is made to assess their deterrent effect, this becomes an important consideration. Naturally, it is easier to assess the material impact of a fine compared to its psychological effect. It is not clear what kind of stigma attaches to these penalties and the whole issue of public condemnation begs a number of questions. For instance, it may be asked whether the subjects of fines are more concerned with peer group reaction or with consumer perception, or whether they worry about either. There is no clear evidence that customers turn away from companies who have been fined or that the latter suffer in any way at the hands of fellow traders or competitors. In the case of major cartels it may make no difference in any case; other traders or consumers may have little choice but to continue to deal with the 'disgraced' parties. Nor is it evident that Community fines attract much attention outside business circles: media coverage is generally limited. The fact that major traders with well-known business names have been prepared to risk the penalties repeatedly suggests that the possibility of adverse publicity does not outweigh the perceived advantages of anti-competitive behaviour.

The material impact of fines is more calculable and in this respect the 10 per cent of turnover maximum may contain a real sting. Even so, it may still be difficult to assess the profitability of restrictive practices[48] and it is conceivable that fines of several million ECU do little to dent the economic position of some undertakings. Members of the Polypropylene Cartel[49] were subject to a total of 58 million ECU in fines: a large figure which, however, has to be seen in the context of a market in Western Europe estimated to be worth 1,500 million ECU.[50] Inevitably much will depend upon the circumstances and in particular on the profitability of the relevant market. Admittedly some restrictive practices are triggered by market problems such as over-capacity, and the Commission has been prepared to take into account the depressed state of an industry in fixing the level of fines.[51] Individual circumstances may also sometimes increase the impact of a fine. In the *Pioneer* case, Advocate General Slynn referred to the possibly difficult position of Musique Diffusion Francaise (MDF):

> it seems established that the fine fixed by the Commission exceeds MDF's working capital; the accounts presented to the Court by MDF disclose a higher proportion of short-term loans .... these factors in my view indicate some reduction in the fine.[52]

The Commission appears to attempt to assess the deterrent impact of its fines and in fact the background to some of the arguments in the *Pioneer* case was the Commission's deliberate policy in relation to the level of the fines. In its pleadings the Commission argued:

> many undertakings persist with practices which they know without doubt to be contrary to Community law because they think that even if fines are imposed on them the profit which they will earn from their illegal conduct will be greater than the fine and that the conduct will therefore have been remunerative. Such attitudes can be discouraged only by the imposition of heavier fines than in the past, at least for recognised infringements.[53]

The appeal to the Court in that case was therefore something of a legal test of that policy, with the result that the Court of Justice approved the Commission's deterrent approach, stating that 'proper application of the Community competition rules requires that the Commisson may at any time adjust the level of the fines to the needs of that policy'.[54]

Exceptionally, a fine may be fixed in some attempt to deprive the offending undertaking of its ill-gotten profit. In the case of *Kawasaki* in 1979,[55] which involved an export ban, the Commission considered the likely effect of the prevention of parallel imports on retail prices. This is a speculative exercise which requires an estimate of the likely volume of sales in the absence of the export ban as well as the resulting retail price which would result from undercutting the appointed distributor. The Commission admitted that such figures could not be determined with any precision and contented itself with a calculation based upon the smallest lowering of retail prices which could have been expected in the medium term. The eventual fine was set at 100,000 units of account, which was the figure set by the Commission for an estimated profit to be made from German sales in the relevant period.[56] Generally, however, the quantum of the Commission's penalties may be viewed as punitive and deterrent rather than redistributive. Any issue of compensation is left as a matter of national law (see the discussion below and in Chapter 9), or more exceptionally may result from a negotiated settlement, when no fine is imposed. So, for instance, in 1987 when the Commission had received a complaint that Angus Fire Armour was abusing its dominant position in the British fire hose market, the matter was resolved by *inter alia* the complainant company receiving an *ex gratia* payment from Angus.[57] Presumably the Commission did not consider that the alleged abuse in this case was especially serious, so that an informal settlement without any sanctions being applied was in order.

Enforcement penalties

There is a second category of pecuniary sanction at the Commission's disposal, designed to reinforce its powers of enforcement and relating therefore to procedural as distinct from substantive offences. Article 15(1) of Regulation 17 allows the Commission to impose relatively small fines of between one hundred and five thousand units of account (ECU) for either intentionally or negligently supplying incorrect, misleading or incomplete information, or refusing to submit to an investigation. This may be in the context of either the notification procedure (incorrect or misleading information; in effect attempting to obtain a negative clearance or exemption by fraud) or of an investigation being carried out by the Commission. Furthermore, the Commission may under Article 16 of Regulation 17 impose day fines (of between 50 and 1,000 units of account per day) on recalcitrant undertakings which refuse to comply with an order to terminate an infringement or to cooperate during an investigation ('periodic penalty payments').

The use of this category of penalties does not on the whole raise such significant legal issues as do fines for substantive infringements, but there may still be problems of interpretation. For instance, when National Panasonic France was asked in 1979 by the Commission about its recommended prices as from January 1976,[58] the company supplied price lists which were being used in 1976, not earlier. The Commission stated that 'the reply in the present tense was intended to give the impression that it related to the whole period covered by the Commission's request' and thus amounted to incorrect information. Although Article 15(1) refers to 'incorrect' information in this context it seems that the subsequent fine was a response to what was perceived by the Commission to be an attempted deception. An innocently mistaken supply of wrong information is unlikely to be covered by Article 15(1) since it would not qualify as intentional or negligent unless it was based upon clear carelessness.

The Commission had not found it necessary to rely on Article 16 until earlier in 1987 when the German company Hoechst refused to submit to an inspection ordered by the Commission (see Chapter 3 in this volume). No doubt real intransigence is more likely in the context of investigations; there is less obvious advantage in holding out against a finding that there has been an established infringement, once rights of appeal have been exhausted.

Temporal considerations

Any fines in relation to substantive infringements of the competition rules must be imposed within a period of five years, a period of limitation laid down under Council Regulation 2988 of 1974. Regulation 17 did not provide for any period of limitation, a fact that formed one of the grounds of appeal by Boehringer Mannheim against the fine imposed in respect of its participation in the Quinine Cartel.[59] This omission was considered at length and sympathetically by Advocate General Gand in his opinion in that case, where he argued:

> This procedure expresses a common truth in legal terms, that is, that time is the great healer, that after a more or less extensive period there always comes a point when, in the relationships of society, the past can no longer be called in question and even if it was wrongful it is better to wipe the slate clean.[60]

The Advocate General recommended that the period of limitation should be five years and this term was in fact adopted in the subsequent Council Regulation. But the Court of Justice was unwilling to lay down any period on its own initiative, taking the view that, although this was a necessary step for reasons of legal certainty, it was only within the competence of the Community legislature.

The five year period is calculated from the date when the infringement was committed or, if continuing or repeated, when it ceases (Article 1(2)). Arguments of fact may arise as to the date of particular infringements or their cessation. For instance, in relation to the Polypropylene Cartel, the Commission rejected arguments that some price arrangements in 1977 were distinct from subsequent pricing agreements and so therefore could not be regarded as finished and time-barred for the purposes of fines.[61] However, the running of time for purposes of limitation will be interrupted by 'any action ... for the purpose of the preliminary investigation or the proceedings in respect of the infringement' as further defined in Article 2(1) of Regulation 2988 (for instance, requests for information or investigations). For 'procedural' infringements, the period of limitation is three years (Article 1(1)(b) of the Regulation).

Another temporal issue centres on the legal disappearance of the party concerned after the infringement has been committed, for example, if a company goes out of business or is merged with or taken over by another company. This raises the question of the liability of successor undertakings. The crucial test, as employed by the Court of Justice, appears to be whether or not a party is an 'economic successor' of the delinquent undertaking in the sense of there being an 'economic and functional continuity' between the two. This is illustrated by the position of SAGA Petrojkemi and Statoil in relation to the Polypropylene Cartel.[62] The former company, which had been a member of the Cartel, had ceased to exist and Statoil had taken over the business complete with its management and employees as a separate identifiable unit within its own corporate structure.[63] The Commission emphasized that the liability to pay the fine imposed on Statoil was vicarious in nature and implied no moral condemnation: 'It is accepted ... that there is no evidence that Statoil continued the infringement' or that 'the acquisition by Statoil was intended to frustrate the application of EEC competition rules'.[64] The problem was to find a legal personality on whom the fine could be imposed: a fine cannot be applied to a division of a company if it is not constituted as a separate legal entity. If Statoil had constituted SAGA as a subsidiary, the fine could have been imposed on the subsidiary alone; but, as Statoil's legal advisers noted, the form of the transfer to Statoil was a matter of luck and circumstance and could depend on the vagaries of national law. On the other hand, the simple purchase of some of the assets of a delinquent company would not result in such vicarious liability.[65] 'Economic continuity' is a difficult concept and much will depend on the particular circumstances of succession. The imperative consideration from the point of view of proper enforcement is to ensure that a simple change of name and legal form do not allow an undertaking to avoid the application of sanctions.[66] Continuity of business and management are likely to prove decisive in this respect.

Finally, it should be noted that payment of fines will be required within a stated period of time, usually three months. Interest may be demanded on the amount of a fine after this period. On the other hand, payment in instalments may be acceptable in cases of hardship.[67]

Notes

1 Cases 25 and 26/84, *Ford v Commission (No. 2)* (1985) E.C.R. 2725.
2 O.J. 1982, L360/36.
3 O.J. 1982, L161/18.
4 Cases 6 and 7/73, *Commercial Solvents v Commission* (1974) E.C.R. 223, 256.
5 Ibid., p. 272.
6 O.J. 1976, L95/1.
7 For instance, *ECS/AKZO (No. 2)*, O.J. 1985, L374/1.
8 Case 27/76, *United Brands v Commission*, (1978) E.C.R. 207, at p. 342.
9 *Continental Can*, (1972) C.M.L.R. D11.
10 Commission, *Fifth Report on Competition Policy*, (1985), point 341.
11 Case 26/75, *General Motors v Commission*, (1975) E.C.R. 1367, p. 1388.
12 See Richard A. Posner, *Antitrust Law: An Economic Perspective* (1976, University of Chicago Press), p. 31 *et seq*. The number of prison sentences has never exceded single figures in any one year.
13 Case 100/80, *Musique Diffusion Francaise v Commission* (1983) E.C.R. 1825.
14 Ibid., p. 1906.
15 Ibid., p. 1947.
16 Ibid., p. 1825.
17 Ibid., p. 1907.

18 Case 19/77, *Miller Schallplatten v Commission* (1978) E.C.R. 131.
19 (1983) E.C.R., p. 1952.
20 Cases 96 etc./82, *IAZ v Commission* (1983) E.C.R. 3369, 3414.
21 Case 26/75, *General Motors v Commission* (1975) E.C.R. 1367, p. 1388.
22 (1975) E.C.R., p. 1389.
23 Cases 32 etc./78, *BMW v Commission*, (1979) E.C.R. 2435.
24 Ibid., p. 2496.
25 *Quinine Cartel*, (1969) C.M.L.R. D41.
26 *Michelin* O.J. 1981, L353/45.
27 Case 85/76, *Hoffmann-la Roche v Commission* (1979) E.C.R. 461.
28 Ibid., p. 470.
29 Ibid., p. 555.
30 Ibid., p. 557.
31 *Toltecs/Dorcet*, O.J. 1982, L379/19.
32 *Vegetable Parchments*, O.J. 1978, L70/54.
33 *BP Kemi-DDSF*, O.J. 1979, L286/32.
34 *Hasselblad*, see note 3, above; see also the examples listed by Bellamy and Child, *Common Market Law of Competition* (3rd ed., 1987), p. 505.
35 *Benelux Flat Glass*, O.J. 1984, L212/13.
36 *Polypropylene*, O.J. 1986, L230/1; (1988) 4 C.M.L.R. 347.
37 *Aniline Dyes (Dyestuffs) Cartel*, (1969) C.M.L.R. D23.
38 *Polypropylene*, O.J. 1986, L230/1; (1988) 4 C.M.L.R., 407.
39 Ibid., p. 408.
40 Case T-3/89, *Atochem v Commission*, judgement of 24.10.91 (not yet reported).
41 *Tetra Pak*, Press Release IP (91) 715, 24.7.91; (1991) 4 C.M.L.R. 660.
42 Case 100/80, *Musique Diffusion Francaise v Commission* (1983), E.C.R. 1825.
43 (1983) E.C.R., p. 1950.
44 Ibid., p. 1909.
45 Ibid., p. 1912.
46 *Benelux Flat Glass*, O.J. 1984, L212/13.
47 Bellamy and Child, op. cit., p. 509.
48 See, for example, *Hasselblad*, O.J. 1982, L161/18.
49 *Polypropylene*, O.J. 1986, L230/1; (1988) 4 C.M.L.R 347.
50 (1988) 4 C.M.L.R., p. 407.
51 For instance, *White Lead*, O.J. 1979 L21/16: 'a market in decline' – therefore no fines.
52 (1983) E.C.R., p. 1952.
53 Ibid., p. 1857.
54 Ibid., p. 1906.
55 *Kawasaki*, O.J. 1979, L16/9.
56 Ibid., p. 16.
57 Commission, *Seventeenth Report on Competition Policy* (1987), p. 75.
58 *National Panasonic France*, O.J. 1982, L21/32.
59 Case 45/69, *Boehringer Mannheim v Commission* (1970) E.C.R. 769.
60 Ibid., p. 721.
61 *Polypropylene*, O.J. 1986, L230/1; above, (1988) 4 C.M.L.R., p. 404.
62 Ibid.
63 O.J. 1986, L230/31–33.

64 (1988) 4 C.M.L.R., p. 401.
65 *NAVEWA/ANSEAU (No. 2)*, O.J. 1982, L325/20.
66 See Advocate General Mayras in Cases 40 etc/73, *Suiker Unie v Commission* (1975) E.C.R. 1663, 2078; Advocate General Rozès in Cases 29 and 30/83, *CRAM and Reizink v Commission* (1984) E.C.R. 1679, 1718.
67 See generally Bellamy and Child, op. cit., pp. 520–521.

8 Substantive antitrust delinquency in the EEC context

In the previous chapter it was argued that a concept of anti-competitive offence had evolved through the Commission's practice of imposing fines; that in defining the kind of market behaviour which deserved a penalty as distinct from being subject to administrative control, the Commission, and to some extent the Court of Justice, had identified a core area of delinquent behaviour which was clearly and wholly unacceptable. What follows is a more systematic review of those practices which have attracted such censure from the Community authorities, as an attempt to delineate in greater detail the content of market delinquency: what is in effect the essential subject-matter of this whole discussion.

What has emerged during the evolution of EEC competition policy is a broad distinction between two kinds of anti-competitive behaviour – the justifiable and condonable on the one hand, the wholly unacceptable on the other. It has taken some time for these categories to be worked out since it was necessary for the Commission to gain some experience of the operation of a number of different practices in a supranational market context.[1] This categorisation may be broadly related to Article 85(3) of the EEC Treaty, the major exempting provision, which allows certain types of *prima facie* restrictive practice to operate since they do possess some clear economic advantages in terms of competition policy provided that they are put into effect under certain conditions. Since the mid-1960s a number of widely used distribution and licensing arrangements and forms of cooperation between competitors have been legally defined in some detail as acceptable for purposes of competition policy.[2] There are still margins of uncertainty, within which the Commission proceeds cautiously on a case-by-case basis (for instance, in relation to some areas of selective distribution, and as regards joint ventures), but to a large extent these issues had been legally clarified by the end of the 1980s. What is not covered by Article 85(3), or is not beyond the scope of the prohibition of Article 85(1) altogether,[3] comprises the heart of anti-competitive conduct: a list of 'classic' infringements which amount to punishably objectionable market behaviour.

In fact, much of this 'core' offensive conduct is listed in the text of Articles 85 and 86. Both of those provisions exemplify their basic statement of prohibition by listing acts which 'in particular' fall foul of the competition rules. The reference to practices such as price fixing, market sharing and discriminatory treatment are the essence of competition policy. It is clear by now that the kind of conduct that will attract full investigation, careful monitoring and likely penalties comprises, with few exceptions, a small number of major categories of infringement: market sharing and related activities on the part of producer cartels; export bans in relation to the distribution of goods; and abusive behaviour by economically dominant companies, especially that designed to eliminate competitors.

Producer cartels

The term 'cartel', originally used to refer to an instrument of international relations for the exchange of prisoners, has been used widely during the twentieth century to describe collusion between market operators, commonly manufacturers, to ensure their respective shares of the market by eliminating competition between themselves and preventing new competitors from entering the market in question. Typical mechanisms for achieving these ends include agreements as to market shares, the fixing of prices and quotas to ensure that members of the group do not compete for greater individual shares, the granting of mutual distribution rights and the exchange of information. The disadvantages for consumers of goods are clear enough – prices may remain artificially high, supplies may be restricted, and there is little scope for innovation and the development of improved products.[4] Manufacturers may be tempted to form cartels in particular when a market is in decline, so as to maintain an existing trading position rather than undertake the risk and commitment of resources involved in diversification. A market in sharp decline may see the emergence of 'crisis cartels', especially when there is limited scope for adaptation. The Commission discovered in the 1960s a strong European predilection for cartels in some markets and one of its tasks has been the gradual dismantling, or at least rendering harmless, of those arrangements. During the 1960s, before the clear lines of competition policy had been laid down, the approach was to negotiate the removal of objectionable features of such combinations. During the last twenty years, however, the Commission has taken an increasingly forceful line, imposing heavy fines in a number of cases, and having to deal with cartels which have been driven 'underground' to engage in secretive collusion. Often these groupings have been broadly international and not just European in character and have involved major multinational companies.

The Commission's earlier softer approach to major cartels is illustrated by its negotiated termination of the Belgian Tile Cartel (*Convention Faience*) in the mid 1960s.[5] A number of horizontal market sharing arrangements were dealt with by the Commission's 'intervention' during the later 1960s,[6] but by the end of the decade, the Commission decided on firmer action in relation to two major international cartels in relation to quinine and aniline dyes, two cases which are also notable as being the first occasions on which fines were imposed under Regulation 17. The producers of aniline dyes had engaged in price fixing collusion. Although the fines are small in comparison with amounts encountered in the 1980s, they signalled the Commission's moral censure and its perception of the seriousness of the infringement. The Commission pointed to the economic size of the members of the cartel, their share of the EEC market in dyestuffs (80 per cent) and the dependence of other industries on these products. Indeed, the companies concerned were significant manufacturers of chemicals on the international market and the list of some of these undertakings now reads ominously as a roll-call of heavyweight antitrust defendants: BASF, Bayer and Hoechst in Germany; Ciba, Geigy and Sandoz in Switzerland; and ICI in the U.K.[7] The parties' subsequent appeal against the Commission's decision was also 'heavyweight' in terms of legal argument, raising a host of substantive and legal questions.[8] Advocate General Mayras referred to an 'exchange of very voluminous written pleadings and oral arguments of unusual length' and stated that the 'information gathered in these cases has been as complete and as detailed as possible, with the collaboration of international experts of unequalled authority and unrivalled intellectual ability and integrity'.[9] The seriousness of the cartel's activities is also reflected in the fact that the German companies had already been subject to proceedings under German law in respect of the same pricing activities in so far as they took effect in Germany.[10]

The decision in relation to the Quinine Cartel[11] also illustrates the significance of such collusion on the European market. There had been longstanding cooperation between manufacturers of quinine and quinidine since shortly before the First World War and the decline in the market for these products in the postwar years had prompted the price and quota fixing arrangements which became the subject of proceedings under both Community and United States law. The members of the cartel were major producers of pharmaceuticals in Germany, France and the Netherlands, and the Commission's investigations had also extended to the activities of purchasers of the products in Italy and Belgium.[12] The appeals against the Commission's decision were again significant in terms of the legal issues raised by the proceedings.[13]

Although the action taken against the quinine and dyestuffs manufacturers signalled a firmer approach to major cartels and was an important step in the developing perception of such practices as Community competition 'offences', other cartel participants were not invariably fined in the following years. In a number of cases in the early 1970s, groups of producers or trade associations were refused exemptions or required to terminate offending arrangements, but not further penalised: the discount agreement of German ceramic tile producers;[14] the exclusive supply and homologation agreement of Belgian central heating manufacturers;[15] the pricing rules of the Dutch Cement Trade Association (Vereeniging van Cementhandelaren);[16] the price control mechanisms of the Dutch association of wholesalers in sanitary ware (GISA);[17] the quota system of the Cementregeling voor Nederland;[18] the activities of the Belgian Cement Cartel (Cimbel);[19] the agreement concerning the supply of gas water heaters in Belgium;[20] the pricing and quota activities of the Nederlandse Cement-Handelmaatschappij, a joint sales agency;[21] and the 'fair trading agreement' of the European glass manufacturers.[22] However, most of these arrangements had been notified under Regulation 17, which in itself precludes the imposition of any fines for operating a restrictive practice while notified (Article 15 of Regulation 17). Moreover, the majority of these practices were not the work of international cartels: most of these decisions relate to collusive activity organised through national trade associations, in particular in Belgium and the Netherlands.[23]

Notification is in some senses an act of good faith, a type of concession indicative of a willingness to be investigated. A more definite sense of delinquency arises from the more furtive and secretive behaviour of cartels, characterised by the legal concept of a concerted practice. In terms of Article 85(1), both the Aniline Dyes and Quinine Cartel were the result of concerted practices, and this was also the case of the next major cartel arrangement to be penalised by the Commission, that of the European sugar producers, in 1973.[24] Around 1968 the Commission became aware of possible collusion within the European sugar industry, through complaints on the part of some sugar consumers about refusals to sell, investigation of a German sugar producer by the Bundeskartellamt, some agreements notified to the Commission, and then in 1969 through an outbreak of 'sugar price war' in the Netherlands. Following investigation, the Commission decided by the start of 1973 that a number of sugar producers had acted together to breach Articles 85 and 86 of the Treaty. The Commission's reaction to these breaches was markedly punitive, imposing fines that totalled nine million units of account; and, according to the undertakings involved, the Commission's procedure had been carried out in 'a systematically punitive spirit'.[25] Although the Court of Justice reduced the amount of the fines, on the ground that the Commission had failed to take into account the way in which the Community organisation of agriculture itself reduced the scope for competition,[26] the case remains an important step in the development of sanctions against cartels. The cartel members were found to have intentionally adopted a number of market sharing and protecting practices in violation of Articles 85(1) and 86, which justified the imposition of fines. A still sterner tone was adopted in the case of the Belgian Wallpaper Manufacturers' Association (*Groupement des Fabricants de Papiers Peints de Belgique*) in 1974.[27] Although the pricing policy of this cartel had been notified to the Commission, doubts were expressed about the companies' good faith, as to whether there had been an attempt to 'conceal the full implications of their market arrangements by providing vague statements and by not disclosing the existence of agreements and written decisions'.[28] But, more sinisterly, the Groupement had engaged in a collective boycott of recalcitrant dealers, a measure which was not mentioned in the notification and which 'is traditionally considered one of the most serious infringements of the rules of competition since it is aimed at eliminating a troublesome competitor'.[29] Moreover, the anti-competitive behaviour was persisted in, even after being condemned by the Nivelle Tribunal de Commerce and then indicated in the Commission's statement of objections.

Not long afterwards, fines were imposed on French mushroom packers for price fixing (though not on the Taiwanese parties to the cartel, who were unlikely to have been aware at the relevant time of the Community's rules concerning extraterritorial jurisdiction).[30] The remaining cases of market sharing by competing firms dealt with in the 1970s were resolved by cease and desist orders, without fines being imposed. During the 1980s, however, a number of significant cartels have been the subject of heavy fines, usually for market sharing or price fixing. Some of these cases have concerned national arrangements which were held to have an impact on trade within the EEC: for instance, the price fixing arrangements of the Dutch association of cigarette manufacturers and importers, the *Stichting Sigarettenindustrie*;[31] the *Meldoc Cartel* of Dutch dairies which engaged in market sharing through quotas and price fixing;[32] and the *Belsaco* case, involving an association of producers of roofing felt in Belgium, who adopted quotas and a common price list.[33] Moreover, a number of cases have also involved truly international groupings comprising companies from a number of countries both within and outside the EEC, such as the *Cast Iron and Steel Rolls Producers Cartel*[34] and the *Woodpulp Cartel*.[35] Most significantly, however, there have been some cases involving major international companies, some with a diverse range of industrial interests, which have repeatedly infringed the competition rules in this way. Two groups of delinquent companies deserve special mention in this respect, one in the chemicals and petrochemicals sector and the other in the area of glass manufacture.

The tendency of companies in the chemicals and pharmaceuticals sector to combine for market sharing objectives was signalled by the exposure of the Quinine and Aniline Dyes Cartels in the late 1960s. Significantly, some of the members of the Aniline Dyes Cartel have reappeared as defendants during the 1980s in connection with two major interrelated cartels in the thermoplastics sector of the petrochemicals industry – the Polypropylene Cartel[36] and the PVC/Polyethylene/LdPE Cartel.[37] Atochem (France), Hoechst and BASF (Germany) and ICI (U.K.) were involved in all three cartels, while Hoechst and ICI were directing members of the polypropylene group. The *PVC Cartel* was unearthed while the Commission was investigating practices in relation to polypropylene and not surprisingly a number of companies were implicated in both infringements (Atochem, BASF, DSM, Hoechst, ICI, Montedison, Shell and Statoil). Some of these companies are therefore at the heart of cartel delinquency, having a clear 'antitrust awareness' and developing covert strategies of collusion, accounting for major shares in the markets concerned and in some cases taking an obstructive attitude towards Commission investigations (Hoechst; see Chapter 8). The level of delinquency is reflected in the severity of the fines, totalling 57,850,000 ECU in the case of the polypropylene producers and 37 million ECU for the PVC group. Another cartel in the chemicals industry was dealt with by the Commission in 1985 (the *Peroxygen Products Cartel*);[38] one of the protagonists in that arrangement, Solvay, reappeared as a defending party in *Polypropylene*, while Atochem was the successor undertaking to another member of the peroxygen group. More recently still, the Commission imposed fines totalling 47 million ECU on three companies operating the *Soda Ash Cartel*: ICI, Solvay and Chemische Fabrik Kalk.[39] This was a long-standing price fixing and market sharing arrangement, which also involved, on the part of ICI, the imposition of contractual ties on customers. All of this suggests a web of habitual restrictive practice within a major industrial sector, based upon a highly conscious, determined and sophisticated policy of maximising profits by means of market sharing.

Another network of recidivist behaviour is evident in the market for flat glass, the subject of a number of Commission decisions during the 1970s and 1980s. In 1984 fines were imposed on four French manufacturers of flat glass who had divided up the Benelux market between themselves.[40] Two of these companies, Saint Gobain and BSN, had been the subject of earlier decisions by the Commission, although no fines had been imposed on those occasions.[41] At the same time the Commission had been investigating the Italian flat glass market; infringements were established in 1981[42] but no fines imposed in view of the short duration of the agreements and their limited application. However, further investigations in 1986 revealed price fixing arrangements which were considered to be contrary to both Article 85 and Article 86 and fines totalling 13.4 million ECU were imposed.[43] This included a fine of 7 million ECU on Fabbricana Pisani, a wholly owned subsidiary of Saint Gobain Industries, the French company fined over a million ECU in 1984 for its participation in the Benelux cartel. Again this whole situation suggests a strong awareness of illegal opportunities on the part of major companies and a willingness to risk repeated sanctions. The furtive nature of this kind of behaviour is also suggestive of a sense of wrongdoing which marks out such companies as major offenders. Investigations and decisions taken during the 1980s, as summarised in Table 8.1, seem to indicate that the Commission is now entering into its stride for purposes of 'cartel-busting'.

Table 8.1 Cartels fined during the 1980s

Cartel	Year of decision	Fine (ECU)
Stichting Sigarettenindustrie (Dutch cigarette manufacturers)	1982	100,000– 425,000
Bureau National Interprofessionel du Cognac (French cognac producers)	1982	160,000
Cast Iron and Steel Rolls producers	1983	1,250,000
Benelux Flat Glass	1984	765,000– 1,450,000
Zinc producers	1984	350,000– 750,000
Peroxygen producers	1985	500,000– 3,000,000
Woodpulp producers	1985	4,125,000 (total)
Polypropylene producers	1986	500,000– 11,000,000
Belgian roofing felt producers (BELASCO)	1986	15,000– 420,000
Dutch dairies (Meldoc)	1986	425,000– 3,125,000
Producers of fatty acids	1987	50,000
PVC producers	1988	37,000,000 (total)
Welded steel mesh producers	1989	9,000,000 (total)

Source: Official Journal of the European Communities, 1982-89.

Export bans

The second major category of antitrust offending occurs in the context of vertical distribution arrangements where distributors are protected from competition within their territory by a variety of mechanisms which prevent 'parallel' importation. Effectively, whatever the means used – contractual obligations, discriminatory pricing, exercise of industrial property rights or insistence on technical standards, for example – what is achieved is a ban on the export of competing goods from one part of the EEC to another. This constitutes, therefore, market sharing at the level of distribution. Such 'absolute territorial protection' of distributors has been firmly and consistently condemned by both the Commission and the Court of Justice since 1966, when such measures were outlawed in the *Consten and Grundig* case.[44]

The successive group exemptions in Regulations 67 of 1967 and of 1983, in relation to exclusive distribution agreements, have emphasised the unacceptability of this kind of practice and export banning cases have consistently attracted fines during the 1970s and 1980s.

By the early 1970s the Commission's view was that 'antitrust awareness' could now be presumed in relation to the prevention of parallel imports. In its *Second Annual Report on Competition Policy*, referring to the fines imposed on WEA Filipacchi for export bans in relation to music records, the Commission stated: 'no firm in the Community can now adduce ignorance of the rule of Community law forbidding contractual restraints on exports'.[45] Thereafter, practices which hindered parallel importing, when detected, were regularly indicted as serious breaches of Article 85(1), justifying the imposition of a fine in many cases – the exceptions tended to be cases in which notification protected the parties, or in which the ban had been quickly removed, as in the case of *AEG Telefunken*[46] in 1974. Typically such apprehended export bans related to consumer goods: electrical goods (Deutsche Philips 1973; AEG Telefunken, 1974; Sperry Rand, 1974; Pioneer, 1979; National Panasonic, 1982; Toshiba, 1991); recorded music (WEA-Filipacchi, 1972; Miller Schallplatten, 1976); drinks (Distillers, 1977; Bell and Teachers, 1978; Moet et Chandon, 1981); cameras and films (Hasselblad, 1981; Konica, 1987); cars and motor cycles (BMW, 1977; Kawasaki, 1978); toys (Polistil/Arbois, 1984; Fisher Price, 1987); pharmaceuticals (Johnson & Johnson, 1980; Sandoz, 1987).[47] In more recent years, business supplies have figured more prominently as the subject of export bans (for instance, farm machinery (John Deere (1985), Sperry New Holland (1985)); correction products (Tipp-Ex (1987)).[48] Most of these fines have been calculated in thousands of ECU, although the more recent fine imposed on Toshiba in 1991 was as much as two million ECU.[49]

There is little doubt, therefore, that in the Commission's view export bans amount to a 'classic' infringement of the competition rules, justifying a penalty. Nor has the Court of Justice done much to modify that perception. Some critics have argued that the Commission's approach is sometimes too inflexible. So, in relation to the 'dual pricing system' used by Distillers for the sale of whisky in the U.K. and on the Continent (an 'export deterrent': whisky for export did not benefit from a discount), Advocate General Warner considered that such measures could come within the terms of Article 85(3), since in practice they did not eliminate parallel imports and covered overseas promotional costs.[50] Despite such views, and criticism of the Commission's approach,[51] the latter has not shifted its ground very much on the condemnation of export deterrents as distinct from bans.[52]

Abuse of dominance

The final major category of restrictive practice which has attracted fines from the Commission comprises certain abuses of market dominance under Article 86 of the Treaty. In both legal and economic terms Article 86 is more problematical: there may be difficult arguments concerning the basic fact of dominance (essentially a question of market analysis) and then the concept of 'abuse' is defined in an open-ended way, so that the lack of predictability may undermine moral justification for using fines. Put another way, 'antitrust awareness' may not so easily be presumed in the context of Article 86.

Although market dominance is the threshold for liability under Article 86, it is the manner in which that position of market strength is exploited which lies at the heart of the condemnation emanating from that provision. It is axiomatic that dominant undertakings may damage competition more seriously than other parties and are therefore considered to have a special responsibility in showing respect for the competition rules. This point has been made by the Court of Justice:

> A finding that an undertaking has a dominant position is not in itself a recrimination but simply means that, irrespective of the reasons for which it has such a dominant position, the undertaking concerned has a special responsibility not to allow its conduct to impair genuine undistorted competition on the common market.[53]

Clearly, there are a variety of ways in which an undertaking may fail to discharge this responsibility; the possible means of abuse are manifold. Yet, over a period of twenty years or so, certain main categories of abusive behaviour have emerged from the case-law of the Commission and the Court of Justice. By analogy with the distinction drawn in section 22(4) of the German GWB between 'exclusionary' and 'exploitative' abuses, some commentators have drawn a line between 'anti-competitive' and 'unfair' practices caught by Article 86.[54]

'Anti-competitive' practices are those which exploit a position of market strength to reduce competition further or eliminate competition altogether; hence the analogy with 'exclusionary' acts which seek to exclude competition from a market. Such exclusionary behaviour is typified by certain anti-competitive methods. One of the most clear-cut is a refusal to supply essential products. The classic case is *Commercial Solvents*,[55] where the sole producer of a raw material refused to supply an existing customer since it wished itself to compete in the market of a derivative product from that raw material; in effect an elimination of competition.[56] An unjustifiable refusal to supply was also established in *United Brands*,[57] in which the Court regarded United Brand's behaviour towards the Danish ripener/distributor Olesen as an excessive response to a competitive threat. Both Commercial Solvents and United Brands were fined. In an Article 177 ruling in 1985,[58] the Court handed down a statement of principle to the effect that:

> an abuse within the meaning of Article 86 is committed where, without any objective necessity, an undertaking holding a dominant position on a particular

market reserves to itself or to an undertaking belonging to the same group an ancillary activity which might be carried out by another undertaking as part of its activities on a neighbouring but separate market, with the possibility of eliminating all competition from such undertaking.[59]

Another group of cases concerns the use of rebates or discounts (feasible because of the firm's dominant position) in order to secure a proportion of the business of customers and prevent other companies from effectively competing for that business. The Commission employed the term 'loyalty rebate' to describe the pricing policy of SZV, a member of the *Sugar Cartel*,[60] which the Court confirmed as an abuse of Article 86. The practice of Hoffmann-la Roche is more notorious in this context: a package of 'loyalty' or 'fidelity rebates', price advantages and related practices (for instance, the 'English clause' which allowed Roche to match more favourable offers from other suppliers), which enabled the pharmaceuticals company to tie its customers to its products.[61] Another practice of this kind was condemned in *Michelin*.[62] There the tyre producer offered turnover related discounts which were considered by the Commission to infringe Article 86. In appealing against its fine the company argued that this was an extension of the principle laid down in *Hoffmann-la Roche* and as such it could not have been aware that it was infringing Article 86. But neither the Court nor Advocate General Verloren van Themaat agreed that Michelin's discounts were so far removed from those condemned in earlier cases so as to absolve it from 'antitrust awareness'.[63] It seems clear from this that any form of discounting or rebating employed by a dominant company in order to preserve a share of customers could fall foul of Article 86.

A number of pricing practices may also be abusive in the sense of Article 86, notably that known as 'predatory pricing', which is designed to drive out a competitor by using very low prices (which dominant undertakings may be in a position to bear). As with other aspects of Article 86, this subject raises difficult issues of economic analysis, and it is not easy to distinguish predatory pricing from normal price competition. Economists are divided on the question: some advocate doing nothing since punitive action may accidentally hit genuine competition; others support a condemnation based on cost-based criteria, but this is not an infallible approach.[64] The Commission took the plunge into this particular pool in 1985 when it decided against the Dutch chemical producer AKZO, holding that it had used a predatory pricing policy to drive the smaller British flour producer ECS out of the flour additives market.[65] The Commission based its decision on documentary evidence which demonstrated 'a firm intention to discipline and, if necessary, eliminate ECS by attacking its base in flour additives in retaliation for its expansion into the plastics sector'.[66] The Commission in this instance eschewed cost-based tests, which were not in any case convincing in the circumstances of AKZO. There was no doubt, as the Court of Justice confirmed, that AKZO had in fact threatened price cuts; but the Court was also willing to go so far as to state, as a matter of principle, that 'prices lower than average variable cost ... by which a dominant undertaking seeks to eliminate a competitor, must be considered as abusive ....'[67] The Court upheld the Commission's finding of predatory pricing, but it was proof of the company's avowed intent to act in this way which made this interpretation of its pricing policy convincing. Arguments about predatory pricing are likely to prove contentious in future cases without the clear evidence of predatory intent which was present in the case of AKZO.[68]

Other pricing practices may come within Article 86 and attract fines. United Brands were penalised, amongst other things, for discriminatory pricing. The company's bananas were sold to customers in different Member States at widely varying prices; the Court of Justice considered that the price differences were artificial and so contributed to a rigid partitioning of national markets.[69] In this situation, it was discrimination based on the nationality of the buyer which was especially offensive and confirmed the abusive nature of the conduct. It is less clear whether price discrimination generally will bring a dominant undertaking within the scope of Article 86. The guiding principle is that any discrimination, to be accceptable, must be objectively justifiable.

Other anti-competitive mechanisms, designed to eliminate or reduce competition, may similarly bring a dominant firm within the terms of Article 86; for instance, the restriction of parallel imports;[70] or unjustified tying arrangements, as exemplified by the recent *Hilti* case.[71] Hilti, a manufacturer of nail guns based in Leichtenstein, was dominant in the supply of magazines for such guns. In order to increase its share of the market for nails, it made the supply of its guns dependent on the purchase of Hilti nails. This tying provision attracted a substantial fine of six million ECU from the Commission[72] since it prevented independent producers of nails for Hilti nail guns from entering the market. The Commission was unwilling to accept the defence that Hilti's conduct was motivated purely by concern for its own safety.

The other main category of abuse under Article 86, comprising behaviour which is 'unfair' or 'exploitative', is based upon a less extensive case-law and indeed in some instances is not easily distinguishable from some of the examples just referred to. However, there have been some cases in which dominant undertakings have been found to have used their position to charge excessively high prices to the clear detriment of consumers. A straightforward instance of this occurred in the case of *General Motors* in the mid-1970s, when the Belgian subsidiary of the car manufacturer was held by the Commission and the Court of Justice to have charged prices which were excessive in relation to the economic value of the service in question – *prima facie* abusive conduct.[73] However, although this principle is clear enough, its application may become bedevilled by problems of market analysis. After the Commission's finding of unfair (excessive) prices was overturned by the Court in *United Brands*, since the Commission had not examined the company's costs,[74] it has been cautious about taking decisions on unfair prices as such. The problem of market analysis was succinctly stated in the Commission's *Fifth Report on Competition Policy* in 1976:

> In proceedings against abuse consisting of charging excessively high prices, it is difficult to tell whether in any given case an abusive price has been set for there is no objective way of establishing exactly what price covers costs plus a reasonable profit margin.[75]

An overview of the case-law under Article 86, and of the Commission's practice in imposing fines for breaches of that provision, therefore suggests that the manifestly abusive behaviour which should be regarded as a punishable offence consists for the most part of anti-competitive conduct clearly designed to eliminate or reduce competition, and is typified by refusals to supply, and rebating, pricing and tying arrangements which effectively prevent competitors from entering into a market. Despite the undoubted difficulties of economic analysis in the establishment of an abuse under Article 86, a 'classic' offence of abusive behaviour can nonetheless be outlined: the exploitation of a position of market strength to keep out or drive out competition. This kind of offensive conduct is illustrated well by another recent case, in which the Commission was also prepared to provide interim relief to the victim company.[76] In this instance, British Sugar, the largest producer of sugar in the U.K., attempted to drive its smaller competitor Napier Brown out of the retail sugar market in Britain, both by refusing to supply the latter with industrial sugar and by using an aggressive pricing policy.[77] British Sugar's tactics towards Napier Brown represented a package of exclusionary measures, some of which (refusal to supply, the offer of 'group commitment bonuses' – similar to loyalty rebates – and overtly discriminatory conditions of supply) were considered by the Commission to be well established abusive practices, so rendering that part of the company's conduct a 'classic' infringement. The Commission conceded that the law relating to predatory pricing was less clear and that its condemnation of the sale of sugar exclusively on a delivered-price basis as an abuse was novel, and took account of the consequently lower level of antitrust awareness in relation to these activities.[78] Considering the size of the company and the seriousness of the infringement, the fine of three million ECU may be considered lenient, but the Commission had also taken into account British Sugar's 'exemplary' cooperation during the proceedings. The essence of the case against British Sugar is stated in the Commission's formulation:

> These abuses were all designed to have the same effects; namely, severely to damage the position of or even eliminate, a newly established competitor on the market.[79]

In general terms, therefore, what is being impugned by many of the fines imposed under Article 86 is a market strategy which is both aggressive and destructive, and all the more so for being engaged in by undertakings who are already in a position of economic strength.

The structure of competition offences: 'classic infringements' and 'antitrust awareness'

Whilst it may be useful to identify the main categories of cases which are likely to attract fines in order to predict the boundaries of liability to penalty under the EEC competition rules, it is also important to extrapolate from such categories the principal unifying elements of liability, as a means of indicating its future development. The three major areas just discussed – manufacturing cartels, export bans in distribution, and abusive conduct on the part of dominant undertakings – should not be regarded as an exhaustive listing. Fines may be and have been imposed in respect of acts which do not fall easily within those categories. In *Windsurfing*,[80] for instance, the parties were fined separately for export bans and for a number of provisions in their patent licensing agreements which restricted the exploitation of the licensed patents, the calculation of royalties and the fixing of license notices. It is necessary, therefore, to identify some more general elements of liability.

Both the Commission and the Court of Justice have stressed the significance in anti-competitive terms of the infringements which have attracted fines. The point may seem obvious, but it informs the concept of 'classic' infringements, whose injury to competition is sufficiently well established, understood and agreed upon to constitute undoubtedly unacceptable conduct. In their simplest forms, agreements to divide markets or prevent parallel imports, or attempts to eliminate competitors or prevent the emergence of new competition are anathema to the achievement of a common or single market. There may be argument around the periphery of classic antitrust behaviour (for instance, in relation to export deterrents, as discussed above), but not as regards the core areas of calculated and damaging anti-competitive conduct which has no redeeming features in economic terms. Once the offending nature of such conduct is established, on the basis of practice and experience, a major element of liability is clear. This empirical mode of legal development also provides a clue to the backward-looking process of definition, whereby the offending conduct is identified according to decisions as to what is punishable.

But liability to penalty also presupposes (from the terms 'intentional' and 'negligent' in Article 15(2) of Regulation 17) a mental element of awareness. And again, in view of the Commission's necessarily empirical approach, it has been necessary to link liability with an awareness not only of the possible damage to competition but also of the clearly established official view that the conduct in question is unacceptable for that reason – what has been referred to in the discussion above as 'antitrust awareness'. Thus it was a number of years before any fines were imposed at all; it was necessary first for the Commission (and the Court) to gain sufficient experience to distinguish the unacceptable and the acceptable and also for this perception to be communicated to market participants. Although the Court has stated a number of times that undertakings do not have to be subjectively aware of the fact that their conduct breached the competition rules, it is necessary for that conduct objectively to have been established as a breach and that this ought to have been known to the parties in question. In this respect, practices such as market sharing within a cartel and the imposition of export bans present no problems; by the early 1970s, knowledge that these were objectionable could be fairly presumed. Nevertheless activity such as predatory pricing is another matter, since the gist of the objection is that low pricing has been used specifically to remove a competitor. There was documentary evidence that this had been AKZO's intention (see above), but not that British Sugar's pricing policy was predatory in this sense; hence the fine in the former case, but not (for pricing policy) in the latter.

In summary, therefore, it may be said that there are two main elements in the Community competition offence (that is, that conduct which is punishable with fines). Firstly, there needs to be a decisively anti-competitive act (as typified by market sharing, export bans or attempts by dominant firms to eliminate competitors). Secondly, there must be a mental element of 'antitrust awareness': that is, that undertakings ought to be aware that the conduct in question is wholly unacceptable. In short, what is penalised is a combination of real harm to conditions of competition and contumacity, and it is clear that the latter element has come to the fore in recent years with the emergence of a number of recidivist cartel members who have participated repeatedly in practices which they in particular know to be strongly condemned.

Notes

1 See D. G. Goyder, *EEC Competition Law* (1988, Oxford University Press), Part 1, on the development of competition policy by the Commission.

2 See Christopher Bellamy and Graham Child, *Common Market Law of Competition* (3rd ed., 1987, Sweet & Maxwell), Chs. 3–7.

3 Applying a test of reasonableness or 'rule of reason', for instance, practices which because of a minimal market share cannot for that reason harm competition very much: see the Commission's Notice on Agreement of Minor Importance of 1986, O.J. 1986, C 231/2.

4 See the Commission's *First Report on Competition Policy* (1972), p. 25.

5 See Goyder, op cit., pp. 54–55.

6 Commission, *First Report on Competition Policy*, pp. 26–27.

7 See also, John Braithwaite, *Corporate Crime in the Pharmaceutical Industry* (1984, Routledge & Kegan Paul), Ch. 5, on the commercial practices of some of these companies.

8 Case 48/69, *ICI v Commission* (1972) E.C.R. 619.

9 *Ibid.*, p. 667.

10 *Ibid.*, p. 703; although the fines imposed by the Bundeskartellamt were later overturned on appeal before the German courts.

11 1969 J.O., L192/5; (1969) C.M.L.R. D41.

12 See (1970) E.C.R., p. 705.

13 Case 41/69, *ACF Chemiefarma v Commission* (1970) E.C.R. 661.
14 J.O. 1971, L 10/15; (1971) C.M.L.R. D6.
15 J.O. 1972, L 246/22; (1972) C.M.L.R. D130.
16 J.O. 1972, L 13/34; (1973) C.M.L.R. D16.
17 J.O. 1972, L 303/45; (1973) C.M.L.R. D125.
18 J.O. 1972, L 303/7; (1973) C.M.L.R. D149.
19 J.O. 1972, L 303/24; (1973) C.M.L.R. D167.
20 J.O. 1973, L 217/34; (1973) C.M.L.R. D231.
21 J.O. 1972, L 22/11; (1973) C.M.L.R. D257.
22 O.J. 1974, L 160/1; (1974) C.M.L.R. D50.
23 Although of a 'national' character, such practices may still have an effect on trade between Member States: see, for example, Case 8/72, *VCH (Cementhandelaren) v Commission* (1972) E.C.R. 977.
24 (1975) C.M.L.R. D65.
25 (1975) E.C.R., p. 2121.
26 Cases 40 etc/73, *Suiker Unie and others v Commission* (1975) E.C.R 1661, 2022.
27 O.J. 1974, L 237/3; (1974) C.M.L.R. D102.
28 (1974) C.M.L.R. D115.
29 Ibid., p. D116.
30 *Re the French and Taiwanese Mushroom Packers*, O.J. 1975, L 29/26; (1975) 1 C.M.L.R. D83.
31 O.J. 1982, L 232/1.
32 O.J. 1986, L 348/50.
33 Ibid., L 232/15.
34 O.J. 1983, L 317/1.
35 O.J. 1985, L 85/1.
36 O.J. 1986, L 230/1.
37 O.J. 1988, L 74/21.
38 *Peroxygen Products Cartel*. O.J. 1985, L 35/1.
39 *Soda Ash Cartel*, (1991) 4 C.M.L.R. 169.
40 *Benelux Flat Glass*, O.J. 1984, L 212/13.
41 O.J. 1974, L 160/1; O.J. 1980, L 383/19; O.J. 1981, L 326/32.
42 *Italian Flat Glass*, O.J. 1981, L 326/32.
43 *Flat Glass*, O.J. 1989, L 33/44.
44 Cases 55 and 58/64, *Consten and Grundig v Commission* (1966) E.C.R. 299.
45 Commission, *Second Report on Competition Policy* (1973), p. 47.
46 Commission, *Fourth Report on Competition Policy* (1974), p. 63.
47 See Bellamy and Child, op. cit., p. 251 *et seq.*
48 Ibid.
49 Press Release, 5 June 1991.
50 Case 30/78, *Distillers v Commission* (1980) E.C.R., p. 2282 *et seq*
51 See, for example, Valentine Korah, *EEC Competition Law and Practice* (3rd ed., 1986, ESC Publishing), pp. 68-69.
52 *Distillers (Johnny Walker) (Red Label)*, O.J. 1983, C 243/3.
53 Case 322/81, *Michelin v Commission* (1983) E.C.R. 3461, p. 3511.
54 For instance, Bellamy and Child, op. cit., p. 410.
55 Cases 6 and 7/73, *Commercial Solvents v Commission* (1974) E.C.R. 223.
56 Note the recurrence of the problem and the Commission's intervention: *Sixteenth Report on Competition Policy* (1986), p. 87.

57 Case 27/76, *United Brands v Commission* (1978) E.C.R. 207.
58 Case 311/84, *Centre Belge d'Etude de Marché-Télémarketing v CLT and IPB* (1985) E.C.R. 3261.
59 Ibid., p. 3278.
60 See Cases 40/73 etc., *Suiker Unie v Commission* (1975) E.C.R. 1663, 2003.
61 Case 85/76, *Hoffmann-la Roche v Commission* (1979) E.C.R. 461.
62 Case 322/81, *Michelin v Commission* (1983) E.C.R. 3461, p. 3511.
63 (1983) E.C.R., pp. 3523, 3546–7.
64 See the Commission, *Seventeenth Annual Report on Competition Policy* (1987), pp. 232–3.
65 O.J. 1985, L 374/1.
66 Ibid., at para. 47.
67 Case C-62/86, *AKZO v Commission*, para. 71 of judgement (not yet reported, but noted, (1991) 4 C.M.L.R. 659).
68 See generally, Bellamy and Child, op. cit., p. 414.
69 Case 27/76, note 57 above, (1978) E.C.R., pp. 298–299.
70 Case 40/73 note 60 above, (1975) E.C.R., pp. 1983–84.
71 Case T-30/89, *Hilti v Commission* (1992) 4 C.M.L.R. 16.
72 O.J. 1987, L 65/19.
73 Case 26/75, *General Motors v Commission* (1975) E.C.R. 1367.
74 (1978) E.C.R., pp. 301–303.
75 At p. 13, point 3.
76 *British Sugar*. 'Had the Commission not issued a statement of objections that led to British Sugar's undertaking a competitor could have been irretrievably removed from the market' (1990) 4 C.M.L.R. 229.
77 O.J. 1988, L 248/41.
78 (1990) 4 C.M.L.R., p. 229.
79 Ibid., p 228.
80 O.J. 1983, L 229/1.

9 The national dimension

The Community legal system is notable for its interlocking of supranational (Community) and national (Member State) procedure in a way that is crucial for the operation of the Community legal order. There is a considerable level of reliance on the Community's part on Member State agencies and at the same time a duplication of interest in that in some situations both Community and national authorities may wish to exercise jurisdiction over the same case. A further aspect of the Community's relations with national authorities arises from the possibility of claiming jurisdiction beyond the geographical boundaries of the Community, for instance over companies based in North America, the Far East or other parts of Europe. Each of these issues, involving the relation between different legal orders, may complicate the working of Community investigation and sanctioning procedures.

Reliance

The Community's reliance on national procedures and agencies arises partly from the geographical overlapping as between the area of application of Community and Member State law. Since Community law necessarily applies within the geographical area of the Member State legal systems it is only sensible for much of it to be given effect by the courts and administrative agencies already in place within those systems. Thus the great bulk of Community law in policy areas such as agriculture and the movement of goods is implemented by customs authorities and other national agencies, such as the British Intervention Board for Agricultural Produce or the German Einfuhr und Vorratsstelle für Getreide und Futtermittel. Moreover the Community law doctrine of direct effect gives national courts an important role in the enforcement of Community law at the initiative of individuals.[1] The overall outcome is a broad dichotomy of functions between Community and national institutions, the former being responsible for the making and interpretation of Community law, the latter for its implementation and enforcement.

Yet in this respect, competition policy provides something of an exception. The Commission's power to deal directly with individual cases, either through voluntary notification or by investigation as described above – a necessary process in order to gain experience, so as to develop policy – derogates from the general practice of reliance on national mechanisms. However, there are practical limits to the extent of this direct dealing and both the practice of disposing of categories of cases by means of group exemptions under Article 85(3) of the Treaty and the Court of Justice's ruling that Articles 85(1) and 86 are directly effective, and so may be applied in national proceedings,[2] are routes by which the Commission's administrative burden may be alleviated. In particular, the direct effect of those Treaty provisions is the basis for the provision of civil remedies such as claims for compensation, which may properly be regarded as part of the sanctioning process in relation to competition policy. But even in those cases in which the Commission itself investigates or imposes a sanction, the ultimate enforcement of decisions to investigate, of orders made in respect of established breaches, or of fines imposed for breaches may depend upon action being taken by national authorities, especially if the undertaking concerned proves to be resistant. There are thus two main contexts in which action taken by Member State authorities needs to be considered: in relation to civil claims arising from breach of the competition rules; and as a back-up for measures ordered by the Commission.

Civil remedies: 'decentralised enforcement'

Since national courts are able to give effect to the prohibitions contained in Articles 85(1) and 86, a number of civil claims are possible before such courts. In the first place the matter could be raised in proceedings relating to contractual questions, when the alleged illegality of an arrangement under either Article 85 or Article 86 is put forward as a means of escaping from contractual provisions. This tactic was used, for instance, by the French company Technique Minière, so giving rise to the reference under Article 177 of the Treaty to the Court of Justice in *Technique Minière v Maschinenbau Ulm*.[3] It is then a question of the relevant national law of contract as to how much of a particular agreement is infected by the taint of illegality under the competition rules, but certainly crucial restrictive clauses may be held to be unenforceable, and in this way the competition rules are being enforced by national courts at the suit of private parties.

In many cases, however, the parties themselves may be only too willing to keep their agreement in operation, but its nullity may be sought by third persons who are adversely affected by it – injured competitors or consumers. Such parties will be seeking a tortious remedy, either in the form of something like an injunction to restrain the illegal activity, or more ambitiously in the form of compensation for loss suffered as a result of the restrictive practice.

Such claims for damages, despite the model of treble damages under United States antitrust law, remain a theoretical rather than an actual addition to the armoury of enforcement in the European context; injunctions on the other hand are much less problematical. As regards the model supplied by American practice, Kaysen and Turner, writing in 1959,[4] commented:

> Private suits are becoming more of an important supplementary enforcement device. They may be the most effective way of policing the multitude of comparatively local and insignificant violations that will tend to escape the glance of federal enforcement authorities, or that even if noticed do not merit the expenditure of limited enforcement resources.

This argument anticipates a similar 'supplementary enforcement' argument which has since arisen in the Community context. Nonetheless, the experience of allowing claims for treble damages under United States legislation (section 7 of the Sherman Act, section 4 of the Clayton Act) suggests that this kind of remedy may be suited to particular classes of case rather than appropriate across the board. There are a number of inherent problems in using claims for compensation as a means of antitrust enforcement, notably the difficulty of quantifying the effects of many anti-competitive acts, and also the lack of self-restraint which may characterise some private claims (what Posner[5] refers to as 'wild and woolly suits'). There is also the problem, in some types of case, of dealing with a multitude of injured parties, whose individual loss is small but whose aggregate injury is considerable; a problem which United States law has dealt with by means of the antitrust class action. Despite these difficulties, private claims in the United States system increased dramatically during the 1960s and 1970s (443 cases filed in 1965; 1162 in 1974), spurred on by the availability of consumer class actions in major price fixing cases. Yet it remains uncertain to what extent the American model is appropriate for the European context. There has always been a tougher tradition of enforcement in the United States, dating back to the end of the last century and which from the beginning contemplated the use of both prison sentences and punitive damages; there was clear legislative provision for civil claims in both the Sherman Act and the Clayton Act; and the development of class actions helped with the problem of dispersed injury. It is not clear that the Community Member State legal systems are nearly so prepared or equipped to embark upon this route of private enforcement.

It is true that the legal framework for private claims exists at the Member State level, at least from the Community point of view. Articles 85(1) and 86 are directly effective and so may be invoked by injured parties before the relevant national courts. The Commission has made it clear[6] that it favours such a legal development. And some national courts have indicated that in principle damages could be claimed. For instance, the German Bundesgerichtshof stated this as a matter of principle in its judgement of 23 October 1979,[7] as did the Commercial Court of Antwerp in *Union de*

Remorquage et de Sauvetage v Schelde Sleepvaartbedrijf in 1965[8] and the English House of Lords in *Garden Cottage Foods v Milk Marketing Board.*[9] Yet an award of compensation has still to be made and a host of legal uncertainties continues to hover around these statements of principle. The Bundesgerichtshof, for instance, qualified its statement by saying that the injured party must have been intended as a specific competitive victim of the defendant's act. The *Garden Cottage* decision was handed down in interlocutory proceedings: the main argument was whether an injunction could be granted, which itself turned on the question whether the plaintiff could ultimately claim damages. But the House of Lords' conclusion that damages could be claimed for a violation of Article 86 as a breach of statutory duty appears somewhat anomalous in the English legal context, where it is very difficult to argue that a breach of the U.K. competition rules will provide the basis for an action for damages.[10] All things considered, there is a list of significant problems which are likely to confront national courts in this situation.

In the first place, there is the issue of expertise, both in relation to Community law (applying Articles 85 and 86) and as regards any economic assessment of injury and its link with the alleged anti-competitive behaviour. The Commission is aware of this potential difficulty and on the basis of a study prepared for it argues that a sizeable proportion of cases would have to remain to be dealt with at the Community level by the Commission. But it also has to be asked whether many potential plaintiffs would have the resources or confidence to mount a private claim, as an alternative to referring the case to the Commission and in effect handing over the fact-finding and presentation of legal argument to the latter's experts. This would surely be a consideration uppermost in the mind of smaller traders with a sense of grievance or concern for the public interest which outweighs their personal material loss. In short it may be questioned whether the cost and effort of private litigation would justify a large number of claims initiated by injured competitors or consumers. The point is well made by Goyder:

> ... the wide powers of investigation and discovery under Regulation 17 and the apparent cheapness of involving its [the Commission] services not to mention the relevant informality with which it could be done have all seemed to both undertakings and their lawyers good reasons for approaching the Commission rather than initiating litigation in national courts ....[11]

A further reason for leaving the matter in the Commission's hands, Goyder points out, is the general enforceability of the Commission's decisions throughout the Community, as compared to the national scope of a judgement from a Member State court (although this is less of an advantage in the case of informal settlement or a comfort letter).

The second main problem is that so much detail needs to be worked out at the national level in relation to this kind of claim that there is a real risk of

uneven development throughout the Member States, even with the availability of the Article 177 reference procedure to obtain guidance from the
Court of Justice. The existing divergence and uncertainties of national law
may ultimately require a harmonising initiative from the Commission if
private claims are going to be brought in large numbers. It would need to be
decided clearly and generally, for instance, whether the intended specific
injury insisted upon by the Bundesgerichtshof in Germany should generally
be a requirement of a national remedy; and what principles should be used to
calculate the quantum of damages – whether, for instance, exemplary damages
should be awarded to take into account the profit of the illegal practice.

Underlying all these considerations, there remains a basic question
concerning the direction being taken in the enforcement of the Community
competition rules. If, as the Commission proposes, some cases should be dealt
with by the Commission at the Community level (the more complex cases, in
economic and legal terms) while others would be dealt with as the result of
private initiative before national courts, it would be undesirable for a different
system of sanctions to be developed and applied as between those two
contexts. Yet this outcome is likely, for the Commission's approach is to
condemn and punish or settle out of court, while national courts would be
involved in providing injunctive relief and awarding compensation. It would
then be necessary to justify a difference of treatment as between those parties
who are fined by the Commission and those whose behaviour may be little
different in substance, but are required to pay damages as a sanction for their
delinquency. Moreover, if the more 'serious' infringements are to be dealt
with by the Commission, presumably third parties injured by such infringements will have to start parallel proceedings before a national court in order to
obtain any compensation, so requiring the devotion of resources to two
separate procedures in relation to the same matter. It should also be borne in
mind that private claims are at the mercy of private initiative, which is likely to
be affected by a host of factors which are less likely to influence the
Commission's decision to take up a case. Unless a convincing division of
labour in terms of a substantively different case-load can be worked out as
between the Commission and Member State courts, it is doubtful whether the
proposal for decentralised enforcement could lead to a satisfactory system of
sanctions within the Community system as a whole.

Measures of cooperation and reinforcement

Regulation 17 provides for the possibility of Member State agencies being
called upon by the Commission to aid the direct enforcement of the
competition rules. There is in the first place an obligation on the Commission's part to keep the relevant national authorities informed about investigations: copies of requests for information must be forwarded (Article 11(2)),
and similarly copies of decisions requiring information must be supplied

(Article 11(6)). If an inspection is proposed, the national authorities must be informed 'in good time' beforehand, and the identity of the Commission's officials participating in the inspection made known (Article 14(2)). Special help may then be required of the national officials. Any 'necessary information' may be requested from the governments or competent authorities of the Member States (Article 11(1)) and the Commission may ask the latter actually to carry out investigations decided upon by the Commission, possibly with the assistance of the Commission (Article 13), but to date the Commission has not availed itself of the opportunity to delegate the conduct of investigations in this way.

Of more immediate significance is the role of the national officials in giving effect to a forcible search of premises under Article 14. These officials must be consulted in any case about any inspection or search (Article 14(4)) and are generally obliged to render any necessary assistance (Article 14(5)). Most importantly, assistance must be rendered if an undertaking refuses to cooperate (Article 14(6)), and this will include facilitating any legal requirements under the relevant national law to carry out a forcible search (see Chapter 3). Although in the *Hoechst* case[12] the Commission had argued that it could carry out searches without the assistance of national authorities and without complying with procedural safeguards under national law, this position was not accepted by the Court of Justice. On the other hand, the national authorities are not able to substitute their own assessment of the necessity for an inspection, a decision which was only reviewable by the Court of Justice. But what may be reviewed by the national authorities is the necessity for specific measures of inspection in relation to the purpose of the investigation. In other words, given that the inspection has been decided upon and may be carried out (if necessary, with local judicial authorisation), the manner in which it is carried out is subject to the relevant national law and the requirements of the latter will be enforced through the observation of the national competition authority. In the words of the Court of Justice:

> the national authorities were entitled to consider ... whether the restrictive measures envisaged were arbitrary or excessive in relation to the purpose of the investigation and to ensure that the rules of national law were complied with in the application of those measures.[13]

The *Hoechst* judgement therefore seeks to delineate a dichotomy of functions as between Community and Member State officials: while the former decide upon and carry out an inspection, the national authorities must provide any necessary assistance (most obviously in obtaining judicial authorisation) and also ensure observance of the applicable local law. The significance of the involvement of national authorities in such inspections largely remains to be tested, as regards both assistance and surveillance – clearly much depends on the level of resistance encountered by the Commission and so far only Hoechst has been noticeably recalcitrant in this way. Neither has there yet appeared any significant divergence of views between the Commission and any Member State authority concerning the former's exercise of its powers.

The other main situation in which the Community is reliant on national procedures is as regards enforcement of the decisions it has taken against undertakings. Orders to terminate infringements or to carry out positive action may be reinforced by the imposition of the Commission's own periodic penalty payments under Article 16 of Regulation 17. It had been unnecessary to resort to these measures until the *Hoechst* proceedings in 1987, when the maximum penalty of 1,000 ECU per day was imposed on the German company. However, the Commission's fines and penalties themselves may need to be enforced ultimately and this will necessarily be a matter of national law. This is provided for in Article 192 of the EEC Treaty, according to the second paragraph of which:

> Enforcement shall be governed by the rules of civil procedure in force in the State in the territory of which it is carried out. The order for its enforcement shall be appended to the decision, without other formality than verification of the authenticity of the decision, by the national authority which the Government of each Member State shall designate for this purpose ....

In England and Wales, for example, the Commission is then able to register its decision imposing the penalty with the High Court, with an order for enforcement from the Government, and the decision then takes effect as an order of the High Court.[14] Ultimate enforcement is thus simply delegated to the appropriate national body and, in view of the obligation contained in Article 192 (such decisions 'shall be enforceable'), failure to enforce a Community penalty would render a Member State in breach of its Treaty obligations. To date there appear to have been no problems in this area.

Overlapping claims

The discussion so far has centred on national courts and authorities acting on behalf of the Community, in a delegated or supporting role. But it should be borne in mind that all of the Member States now have a system of protection of competition at the national level and some restrictive practices may offend both Community and national rules on competition. At the time when the Community rules first came into force, the level of national intervention was variable, ranging from the vigorous German system of control established in the 1950s[15] (an outcome of its postwar occupation: the American influence is noticeable) to the non-existence of any kind of competition law in Italy.[16] In recent years a number of West European countries have reformed their existing law or introduced new laws – for instance, Spain, Italy, Sweden and Ireland[17] – and much of this new legislation has used the Community approach to the control of restrictive practices as a model. The general position, therefore, is that competition is protected in tandem by national and Community processes, the latter being concerned with anti-competitive behaviour with a Community dimension, which in the wording of Articles 85 and 86 'affects trade between Member States' and injures 'competition within the common market'.

However, the Community element in a restrictive practice has been widely interpreted by both the Commission and the Court of Justice[18] to include some activities that at first sight appear not to extend beyond the boundaries of one State. For instance, in the *Dutch Cement Dealers' Case*[19] the Court of Justice stated that an agreement contained within the territory of one Member State but extending over the whole of that territory by its very nature has the effect of reinforcing a compartmentalisation of markets on a national basis and so impedes the aims of the EEC Treaty. There is no doubt then, that the Community rules may apply to some 'domestic' arrangements, just as the national rules may apply to international or Community-wide practices in so far as they damage competition within a particular country.

The legal implications of this overlapping of jurisdiction was confronted by the Court of Justice in 1969, when a number of issues were put to it for clarification by the Kammergericht of Berlin in a reference for a preliminary ruling.[20] In 1967 the Bundeskartellamt had fined a number of German chemical manufacturers (BASF, Bayer, Hoechst, Cassella-Farbwerke Main- kur – none other than members of the Dyestuffs Cartel) for their involvement in price-fixing agreements in relation to aniline dyes. In the meantime, the Commission had independently started its own investigation and the parties, led by Bayer's director Walt Wilhelm, sought to argue that two sets of proceeding in relation to the same practice, and the possibility of two sets of fines, was contrary to the principle of justice enshrined in the phrase 'non bis in idem': that is, that a person should not be punished twice for the same act. The German, Dutch and French Governments intervened in the argument to urge that the national procedures should still be allowed to operate, even if the matter was or could be the subject of Community proceedings. This view was accepted in principle by the Court of Justice, provided always that this did not prejudice the full and proper application of the Community rules:

> ... this parallel application ... can only be allowed in so far as it does not prejudice the uniform application throughout the common market of the Community rules on cartels and of the full effect of the measures adopted in the implementation of those rules.[21]

The principle established by the Court is therefore that national authorities should defer if necessary to the Community interest and take 'appropriate measures' in the event of a conflict or possible conflict between decisions at the two levels.[22] But it needs to be borne in mind that *different* decisions need not be incompatible. It is possible, for instance, for a restrictive practice not to injure inter-Member State trade in a significant way, yet be objectionable at the national level.[23] A problem is most likely to arise if a Member State authority takes a more lenient (or possibly more repressive) approach, which undermines the effectiveness of the Community rules. It is quite possible in principle for the Community and national impact of a restrictive practice to be different.

This kind of issue was in fact contemplated by the Treaty drafters, who provided in Article 87(2)(c) for Council regulations to determine the relationship between national and Community competition law. The Court's statement in the *Walt Wilhelm* case were made in the absence of such a regulation and of course without prejudice to any such measure, but in the event has served instead as another way of dealing with the matter.

The second main point raised in the *Wilhelm* ruling concerned the application of penalties under the two systems – the problem of 'double jeopardy'. Here justice would appear to require that an earlier penalty, in respect of substantially the same act, be taken into account when the second penalty is being considered. This is suggested by the Court of Justice in the *Wilhelm* case as a requirement of natural justice.[24] The same principle is laid down explicitly in Article 90 of the Coal and Steel Community Treaty, in relation to penalties imposed by the Commission under the provisions of that Treaty (see the discussion below in Chapter 10). The last part of Article 90 requires the Commission to be informed of any national administrative or judicial action taken against an undertaking in respect of the same matter and to take account of any final decision on the case at the national level in determining any penalty of its own.

What is important in such cases is to determine whether the second penalty is being applied in respect of the same offending conduct: that is, the same practice and a similar impact. In the case of Member State law this is likely to be the case, given some identity of geographical impact. The injury to competitors in Germany, for instance, is likely to be subsumed within the injury to competition within the Community as a whole. However, in the case of a penalty imposed in a non-Community State, there may be a different anti-competitive impact to be taken into account and this may justify an additional penalty. This point was made in the appeal against the Commission's decision on the *Quinine Cartel*,[25] when Boehringer Mannheim argued that the Commission should have taken into account a fine already imposed on the company under United States law.[26] However, in the view of the Court of Justice, the two 'convictions' (that is, under American and Community law) differed as regards both their object and their geographical emphasis. The United States conviction:

> related to a wider body of facts and was directed in particular against the agreement on quinquina bark and the acquisition and division of American strategic stocks by the cartel, and the successive application of particularly high selling prices in the United States ....[27]

In other words, the European and American consequences of the Cartel's activities constituted separate 'offences' justifying separate penalties. The argument was put succinctly by Advocate General Mayras: '... the territorial effect, potential or real, is one of the ingredients of the infringement. Indeed, it is an essential ingredient'.[28] And furthermore:

> In the United States ... the only acts which can be considered are those which come within Federal law and which are detrimental to the interests of the Union; similarly, the Commission in Brussels can only consider ... acts which, because of their purpose or effect, would adversely affect competition inside the common market. The fact that the agreements in question would be the same is not sufficient to establish that the acts are identical.[29]

This represents a clear and persuasive analysis of the application of the 'double jeopardy' principle. 'Non bis in idem' should apply if there is an *identity of act* underlying the two sanctions. This is likely to be the case as between Community and Member State proceedings; but may well not be the case as between Community and third State proceedings. Territorial economic impact is decisive in this respect.

Extra-territorial jurisdiction

A different problem involving the relation between the Community and national legal systems arises from the assertion of jurisdiction over parties involved in restrictive practices who are situated outside the territory of the EEC. It is not surprising that this issue should arise since it was inevitable that some of the most significant breaches of the competition rules would be perpetrated by members of international cartels, sometimes based in other major trading countries in Western Europe, North America or the Far East. The principal basis for the exercise of jurisdiction is territorial and there is of course no legal problem if an extra-Community firm enters into an agreement directly with a company based in the territory of the EEC or carries out business through a branch there, so acting directly on Community territory. However, problems of jurisdiction may arise if it is disputed factually whether a company was territorially present in any way in the EEC, or if a company outside the EEC acts through another legal person, usually a subsidiary company, based on Community territory.

In discussing this question a distinction may usefully be drawn between two categories of jurisdiction: prescriptive and enforcement. Prescriptive jurisdiction concerns the applicability of rules – in this context, whether Community rules may apply beyond the territory of the EEC. The answer to this question has been clear enough as a matter of Community law: if a company in Japan, for example, enters into an agreement with a company in Belgium and that agreement has an adverse effect on competition within the EEC, then the Japanese company is in breach of Article 85 of the Treaty. The Court of Justice made such a ruling in the *Béguelin* case,[30] in which it stated:

The fact that one of the undertakings which are parties to the agreement is situated in a third country does not prevent application of that provision [Article 85] since the agreement is operative on the territory of the common market.[31]

At first sight this is no more than an application of the so-called objective territorial principle of jurisdiction, which is based on the fact that an action is consummated on the territory in question. In general terms, this approach is acceptable for purposes of international law, as indicated by the International Court of Justice in its well-known *Lotus* judgement.[32] However, the International Court in the *Lotus* case was concerned with the extra-territorial effect of criminal law and, as has already been seen, it may be open to argument to what extent breaches of competition rules may be equated with criminal offences. It is probably sufficient to show that what is involved is an exercise of *repressive* jurisdiction, whether formally categorised as criminal or administrative. ICI, in its appeal against the Commission's decision in the *Dyestuffs Cartel* case[33] argued that the *Lotus* principle was not relevant to competition proceedings, but Advocate General Mayras was not convinced. He urged that the relevant concept was one of 'reprehensible conduct' which would include breaches of competition law:

> For in most developed and industrialised countries substantive law forbids and suppresses, either by penal or administrative means, agreements or practices which adversely affect competition.[34]

In practice the Commission has sought to apply the EEC competition rules to parties outside the Community and although this policy has been legally challenged on a number of occasions, it has been approved by the Court of Justice. In the majority of cases the Court has justified this exercise of jurisdiction by imputing the behaviour of subsidiary companies based territorially within the Community to parent companies beyond its borders through the concept of 'unity of economic group': the subsidiary effectively had no choice, its market behaviour was controlled by the parent company and so, in a sense, the latter was directly involved in the breach and so acting within the Community.[35] There has also been some attempt to justify extra-territorial jurisdiction in this context by resorting to the 'effects' doctrine, favoured in the law of some national systems, such as the United States,[36] Switzerland[37] and Germany.[38] This principle was espoused by Advocate General Mayras in the *ICI* case in the form of allowing acts which have a direct, foreseeable and substantial effect on competition within the Community to supply a basis for extra-territorial jurisdiction,[39] and this view has been regularly asserted by the Commission itself[40] and has more recently been accepted by the Court of Justice in its judgement on the appeal against the Commission's *Woodpulp Cartel* decision.[41] The Court stated in its judgement that:

The decisive factor is ... the place where it [the agreement] was implemented ... The producers in this case implemented their pricing agreement within the common market. It is immaterial in this respect whether or not they had recourse to subsidiaries, agents, sub-agents, or branches within the Community in order to make their contacts with purchasers within the Community.[42]

Advocate General Darmon commented, in his opinion, that there was no rule of international law which could be relied upon against the criterion of direct, substantial and foreseeable effect.[43] Over the years, therefore, the Court of Justice has used both the concept of imputability ('unity of economic group') and the doctrine of effects to justify the exercise of extra-territorial jurisdiction, and has satisfied itself of the compatibility of this approach with general international law.

However, it is one matter to assert jurisdiction, but another to enforce it against particular individuals, for instance by making the party in question abide by court orders or submit to sanctions. In practice, the more crucial question is therefore whether Commission orders or fines may be enforced against parties not present on the territory of the EEC. This question of *enforcement* jurisdiction has not always been clearly distinguished in discussion of the extra-territorial application of Community competition rules. Advocate General Mayras drew the distinction in his opinion in the *ICI* case and argued that while the Community did have an extra-territorial prescriptive jurisdiction (*jurisdictio*) it could not insist on such enforcement (*imperium*) beyond its boundaries:

> Whether it be criminal law or, as in the present cases, administrative proceedings that are involved, the courts or administrative authorities of a State – and, *mutatis mutandis*, of the Community – are certainly not justified under international law in taking coercive measures or indeed any measure of inquiry, investigation or supervision outside their territorial jurisdiction where execution would inevitably infringe the internal sovereignty of the State on the territory of which they claimed to act.[43]

Advocate General Mayras did not, however, regard the imposition of a fine, as distinct from its recovery, as an exercise of enforcement jurisdiction.[45] Whether or not it is agreed that the decision to impose a fine is prescriptive, in practical terms the important question is whether it may be recovered and there it must be recognised that nothing is legally possible if a company wholly outside the territory of the Community refuses to comply.

To date, compliance with orders or fines imposed by the Commission has not raised any major problems, beyond the challenge of the legality of some of these decisions before the Court of Justice. It is worth noting, however, that some States have reacted strongly in the past to the extra-territorial imposition of sanctions on their own nationals. A notable instance was the Swiss protest at the American judgement in the *Swiss Watchmakers' Case*[46] which ordered the Swiss Federation to annul certain contracts and terminate restrictions on exports to the United States, even though they were in conformity with regulations issued by the Swiss authorities. The diplomatic intervention of the Swiss Government led to a revision of the judgement. Such an aggressive stance on extra-territorial jurisdiction can be counter-productive and lead, for instance, to legislative counter-measures such as the U.K. Protection of Trading Interests Act of 1980. This sensitivity has been recognised by the Community bodies. In its decision in *Eastern Aluminium*,[47] the Commission indicated that it was willing to take into account, where appropriate, the fact that its decision may require undertakings to act in a way contrary to their own national law or that Community orders might adversely affect important interests of a non-EEC State.[48] In practice many States, and the Community, now recognise that it is sensible to follow a principle of international comity in relation to possible conflicts of jurisdiction. There are now consultation mechanisms, for instance under the OECD Council Recommendation of 25 October 1979 concerning cooperation on restrictive business practices affecting international trade, and these were used in the course of the Commission's investigation of the *Woodpulp Cartel*.[48] Ultimately, any enforcement of a fine or order against a recalcitrant undertaking in a non-EEC country may require the assistance of the authorities of that State, and assertive claims of jurisdiction are unlikely to gain such assistance.[50]

Another solution which may be available in some cases, would be to take enforcement action against assets which are present in the territory of the State seeking enforcement. This would be a real possibility in the case of the European Community since a large number of multinational companies based outside the Community act through subsidiaries established on Community territory, who would therefore be vulnerable to measures of enforcement. This presumably explains the high level of compliance. Nonetheless, 'comity' may still come into the picture, if any vigorous measures of enforcement are strongly contrary to important economic interests of non-EEC countries.

Notes

1 On the doctrine of direct effect, see Trevor Hartley, *The Foundations of European Community Law* (2nd ed., 1988, Oxford University Press), Ch. 7.

2 See, for example, Case 127/73, *BRT v SABAM* (1974) E.C.R. 313.

3 Case 56/65, (1966) E.C.R. 234.

4 C. Kaysen and D.F. Turner, *Antitrust Policy* (1959, Harvard University Press), p. 257.

5 Richard A. Posner, *Antitrust Law: An Economic Perspective* (1976, University of Chicago Press), p. 228.

6 For instance, *Fifteenth Annual Report on Competition Policy*, p. 48 et. seq.

7 *BMW*, 1980 *Wirtschaftsrecht*, 392.

8 *Union de Remorquage et de Sauvetage v Schelde Sleepvaartbedrijf* (1965) C.M.L.R. 251.

9 *Garden Cottage Foods v Milk Marketing Board* (1984) A.C. 130.

10 See Christopher Bellamy and Graham Child, *Common Market Law of Competition* (3rd ed. 1987, Sweet & Maxwell), p. 459.
11 D. G. Goyder, *EEC Competition Law* (1988, Oxford University Press), p. 353.
12 Cases 46/87 and 227/88, *Hoechst AG v Commission*, (1989) E.C.R. 2859; (1991) 4 C.M.L.R. 410.
13 (1991) 4 C.M.L.R. 468–9.
14 The European Communities (Enforcement of Community Judgements) Order 1972, S.I. 1590.
15 Gesetz gegen Wettbewerbsbeschrankungen (GWB) 1957.
16 See Corwin D. Edwards, *Control of Cartels and Monopolies: An International Comparison* (1967, Oceana), Ch. 1, on the postwar legislation in this field.
17 See Maria G. Rubio de Casas, 'The Spanish Law for the Defence of Competition', 11 (1990) E.C.L.R. and Supplement 1; Alessandra Mancini, 'The Italian Law in Defence of Competition and the Market', 12 (1991) E.C.L.R. 45, and Supplement 1; Carl Svernlov and Leif Gustafsson, 'Stricter Anti-trust Enforcement in Sweden', 12 (1991) E.C.L.R.; Alec Burnside and Eugene Stuart, 'Irish Competition Law – Moving Towards the European Model', 13 (1992) E.C.L.R. 38.
18 Bellamy and Child, op. cit., p. 105 *et seq.*
19 Case 8/72, *Cementhandelaren v Commission* (1972) E.C.R. 977.
20 Case 14/68, *Walt Wilhelm v Commission* (1969) E.C.R. 1.
21 Ibid., p. 14.
22 Ibid., pp. 14–15.
23 Cases 253/78 etc., *Procureur de la République v Giry et Guerlain* (1980) E.C.R. 2327.
24 (1969) E.C.R. p. 15.
25 J.O. 1971, L282/46; (1972) C.M.L.R. D121.
26 Case 7/72, *Boehringer Mannheim v Commission* (1972) E.C.R. 1281.
27 Ibid., p. 1289.
28 Ibid., p. 1301.
29 Ibid., p. 1302.
30 Case 22/71, *Béguelin Import v G.L. Import-Export* (1971) E.C.R. 949.
31 Ibid., p. 959.
32 *The Lotus* (France v Turkey), Pub.PCIJ (1927), Series A, No 10.
33 Case 48/69, *ICI v Commission* (1972) E.C.R. 619.
34 Ibid., p. 694.
35 See in particular Case 48/69, *ICI v Commission* (1972) E.C.R. 614; Cases 6, 7/73, *Commercial Solvents v Commission* (1974) E.C.R. 223.
36 *Swiss Watchmakers' Case (U.S. v Watchmakers of Switzerland Information Centre)*, 133 F. Suppl. 40 (1955), 134 F. Suppl. 710 (1955) (United States);
37 Article 7(2)(b) of the Federal Law on Cartels, 20 December 1962 (Switzerland);
38 Article 98(2) GWB, 1957.
39 (1972) E.C.R., pp. 695–6.
40 See, for example, Commission's *Eleventh Annual Report on Competition Policy* (1981), p. 39.
41 Cases 89 etc./85, *Ahlström and others v Commission* (1988) E.C.R. 5193.
42 Ibid., p. 5243.
43 Ibid., p. 5227.
44 (1972) E.C.R., p. 695.

45 This was also the Commission's argument; ibid., p. 633.
46 See note 36 above.
47 O.J. 1985, L92/1.
48 Ibid., p. 48.
49 See (1988) E.C.R., p. 5244.
50 For a useful general overview of developments at both an international and national level, see Ian Brownlie, *Principles of International Law* (4th ed., 1990, Oxford University Press), pp. 307–309.

10 Delinquency, criminality and economic regulation

The foregoing discussion has presented an account of a sophisticated system of legal control of business activity at an international (or, bearing in mind the specifically European Community context, supranational) level. At the national level competition law already exemplifies one of the most fully developed mechanisms of economic regulation and it is therefore not surprising that in the European Community context it also provides the principal arena for direct intervention in economic life. The subject is, however, more than just one of economic regulation, which can be achieved by a variety of means. The kind of intervention which has been provided for in the field of competition policy has a direct and intrusive quality and a cutting edge which transforms it into a distinctive instrument of control. Its imperative prohibitory character in relation to certain types of practice and its provision for direct investigation and for punitive sanctions is suggestive of the kind of legal control encountered in the field of criminal law. Thus, leaving aside the more specific legal issues which arise in this field and which have been debated in the previous chapters, there are some underlying theoretical questions concerning the juridical character of this system of control which also deserve discussion. At a very general level there is the question of the relation between economic regulation and repressive systems of legal control, summed up in the enquiry concerning the appropriate use of criminal sanctions for purposes of economic regulation. This general question begs a number of further questions regarding the concept of criminal law and procedure (already discussed at a number of points in relation to the distinction between 'criminal' and 'administrative' procedures) and regarding the characterisation of undesired behaviour as 'criminal', 'delinquent', or whatever else. These are significant issues of legal theory, not just in themselves but also as a means of providing a better understanding of some of the more specific questions already raised. Working out rights of defence, for instance, inevitably takes the debate into the theoretical realm of definition and concepts and it would be a considerable omission in a work of this kind not to attempt to provide some kind of answers to these theoretical questions.

It is axiomatic in any system of economic regulation that many forms of economic and business activity will be ruled to be unacceptable. The objectionable nature of such activity varies greatly from between the morally repugnant at one end of the spectrum to the pragmatically inconvenient at the other. The traditional condemnation of systems of criminal law relates to acts which are widely regarded as morally bad – typically violent or psychologically damaging behaviour and that which demonstrates a clear disregard for others' enjoyment of peace and property. Much of this is summed up in the classic 'liberal' doctrine which talks in terms of clear harm to others as a basis for criminalising certain behaviour.[1] The problem with the control of economic life is that much of it is concerned with behaviour which is morally neutral, in the sense that its objectionable character arises not from pathological human traits but from the exigencies of economic policy which may be far from universal in terms of both time and place. The protection of competition itself provides a clear example of this fact, in that not only is it a desideratum of a certain politico-economic creed (liberal capitalism), but even within the scope of that ideology its imperative character is (or has been until recently) variable, being vigorously asserted in some legal systems to the extent of using the criminal law, but weakly controlled if at all in other systems. But it is not even necessary to rely on competition as an example of the shifting grounds for condemnation in the economic field. It is useful to recall that some behaviour which is now generally accepted as wholly unacceptable, and therefore a suitable subject for criminalisation, was not regarded as such a few centuries ago. Fraudulent dealing, now a significant type of criminality in many legal systems, both in terms of its occurrence and perceived seriousness, is a relatively late arrival in the criminal calendar, and at the beginning of the eighteenth century was as much regarded as a matter of clever gain as moral objection.[2] All of this illustrates the essential dilemma in working out the mechanisms of economic regulation. Criminalisation is so highly suggestive of a sense of moral repugnance that there is a natural restraint in acceding to its use in many contexts. Just as the common reaction three hundred years ago may have been amazement that a person should be made a criminal for making a fool of another by dishonest stratagems, so the contemporary view in many quarters is that anti-competitive behaviour is not something which can be readily accepted as criminal. To many, the objection may be no more than instinctive, a feeling that distorting or preventing competition is so qualitatively different from intentional personal violence as to require a legally distinct form of condemnation. This is one line of argument which requires further consideration. There is also another argument which is based on practical and policy considerations and is concerned with the effectiveness of criminal law as a means of social control: whether there is a justification in terms of resources and efficiency. A sub-text of this line of argument raises the question of whether the criminal sanction is justifiable in any case. This is the 'abolitionist' stance, that the use of criminal law is fundamentally flawed as an unacceptable use of power and that attention should be given to less repressive mechanisms.[3] These arguments may be used as a broad critique of the processes of regulation which are being developed in a field such as competition policy. But there is also, in the specifically European Community context, a further level of argument, which relates to the political acceptability of the mechanisms and powers of a system of criminal law being used beyond the national level, and it should be asked whether the official categorisation of such power as being of a 'non-criminal law nature' has much meaning beyond the rhetorical and what is the practical significance of the development of European Community investigations, hearings and sanctions.

Economic control and penality: the model under the Coal and Steel Community

It should be borne in mind at this stage that the development of economic control in the context of EEC competition policy represents the most significant but not a unique experience in the use of investigations and sanctions at the Community level. Already from the 1950s, similar powers had been laid down in the more specific sector covered by the European Coal and Steel Community and since these pre-date the competition procedures they should in some respects be viewed as an earlier model. The Commission also has analogous powers in the fields of land and maritime transport[4] under the EEC Treaty, but these are so clearly modelled on the competition procedures as not to present very much new of either theoretical or practical interest. In this context the investigation procedures laid down under the EEC Treaty into alleged anti-dumping activities,[5] which can lead to the imposition of 'duties' which have a largely corrective function, should also be noted. In so far as there is a replication in these areas of the powers and procedures to be found in the field of competition law there would be little point in carrying out a detailed examination, since the most significant legal issues will have already been discussed in the context of the latter. Something may, however, be said about some of these procedures in other sectors in so far as they supply a differing model of economic control and present something of an alternative to the more repressive approach which has been examined so far in the field of competition policy generally.

A brief survey of the procedures laid down under the Coal and Steel Community Treaty suggests a mixture of approaches, sometimes approaching the rigour of what is allowed for under Regulation 17 of 1962, but in other places resorting to a model which is less obviously penal. It may be useful at this point to draw a theoretical distinction between two significant methods of economic regulation, both of which have a prohibitory and repressive character, yet which employ sanctions of a different nature. The first sanction in question is the familiar penal measure well-established in the field of criminal law. It is punitive in the sense that it comprises a condemnation for rule-breaking and sets out to inflict unpleasantness, both as a means of reinforcing respect for the rules which have been breached and of dissuading further breaches in the future; in short, it has both retributive and deterrent characteristics.[6] This kind of measure is represented commonly in the context of economic regulation by the fine, a pecuniary penalty. But the term 'fine' is sometimes used – both as a measure of national criminal law and in the Community system – to describe a sanction of a subtly different order. In such cases there is a superficial appearance of penality, in that what is involved is the infliction of an unpleasant measure as a response to rule-infraction. Moreover, there may again be a dissuasive objective. Yet a convincing retributive element is lacking from this kind of sanction which may perhaps be better described as redistributive in function. The most useful example is probably that kind of taxation or levying which has a significantly corrective element. Many fines are in substance levies of such a kind, for example those imposed for parking a motor vehicle in a prohibited zone, or for being in possession of a library book which is overdue. Paying an excess rail fare is a measure of a similar kind, though never ordinarily called a fine or a levy. In all of these cases, rules have been broken and an undue advantage gained, which is then corrected or redistributed by the fine, levy, charge or tax. But it may not be appropriate to view such measures as 'penal' in the fullest sense of that term, since there is a significant aspect of disapproval and stigma lacking in such cases and the sanction is more redolent of an economic transaction, and of 'paying a higher price' for going beyond the norm. Certainly in practice many such payments are handed over with a degree of equanimity which undermines any sense of a penal experience. For purposes of this discussion the latter kind of sanction may be conveniently termed a levy.

A brief listing of the 'fines' which may be imposed under a number of Coal and Steel Community procedures[7] indicates how some may be categorised as pecuniary penalties (that is, as penal in character) while others are more in the nature of a levy (that is, having a primarily redistributive and non-stigmatising impact). This exercise will also serve to place in perspective the apparently wide fining powers available to the Commission directly under the Coal and Steel Community Treaty itself.

Article 47: fines and periodic penalty payments may be imposed in respect of obstructive conduct in relation to the Commission's investigations or checks for information.[8] These are comparable to the procedural fines available to the Commission under Article 15(1) of Regulation 17 and penalty payments under Article 16.

Article 54(6): fines may be imposed for disregarding a prohibition on using certain resources available through or covered by loans and guarantees made by the Community. The fine may not exceed the amount of money improperly used. Here the measure is some way removed from a penalty and is perhaps closer to a quasi-contractual recovery of money unlawfully held.

Article 58(4): fines may be imposed for exceeding production quotas laid down by the Community, but may not be fixed higher than the value of the excess tonnage. This is an area in which a number of fines have been imposed, especially in relation to steel quotas,[9] but they are usually fixed at a general level (100 ECU for every tonne in excess of the quota). Although this general level of fine may be doubled for repeated infringements or if the excess is more than 10 per cent,[10] so importing a penal element into the fine, the ceiling of the fine is fixed at the value of the excess tonnage, so that the producer in question is not likely to lose money on balance in the end.

Article 59(7): fines for not complying with prescribed production or deliveries, to deal with shortages. The fine may not exceed twice the value of the amount prescribed. There is some similarity here with punitive compensation since the fine is related to the amount of loss suffered through the failure to produce or deliver.

Article 64: fines for breaches of decisions concerning pricing. Discriminatory pricing or unfairly competitive pricing may be fined, up to a maximum of twice the value of the sales effected in disregard of pricing decisions taken by the Commission. These measures are therefore similar to those taken under Article 59(7).

Article 65(5): fines in relation to restrictive practices. This is where the closest parallel would seem at first sight to lie with Article 85 of the EEC Treaty. However, the maximum fine may not exceed twice the amount of turnover in the products subject to the agreement, unless there was an intention to restrict production, investment or technical development, in which case it may rise to 10 per cent of the undertaking's annual turnover. On the whole therefore these fines do not have the same penal range as those which are provided for in Regulation 17 and in fact they are quite rare.[11]

Article 66(6): fines in relation to various infringements as regards concentrations – for example, an unauthorised concentration subsequently approved must be subject to a fine of 5-10 per cent of the value of the assets acquired or regrouped, which is rather like a levy paid on the approval.

Article 68(6): fines for non-compliance with recommendations concerning wage levels. The maximum level is set at twice the amount of the saving in labour costs.

Taking an overall view therefore of the Commission's fining powers in this context, it can be seen that they are very much much related to the level of unauthorised gain and the predominant purpose is to recover the amount of unjustifiable profit, with in some cases the possibility of a penal doubling of that amount, suggesting analogies with measures such as punitive damages or interest on outstanding tax bills. Since in practice the greatest number of fines is imposed for exceeding production quotas, where no real penal payment is involved, the general fining practice of the Commission in this area lacks the punitive impact which is increasingly the objective of using fines in the field of competition policy.

Although care should be taken not to generalise too far in discussing these coal and steel sanctions, there is an overriding sense of recovering undue gain and any penality is strictly linked to the amount of that gain. The terms 'compensation' and 'damages' are suggestive of private claims, which is why the concept of a levy, connoting the idea of a public claim for redistributive payment, is put forward in this context to describe the nature of these sanctions. Certainly, there are analogies with the provisional and definitive anti-dumping levies which can be imposed under the EEC Treaty to protect the Community market from products exported from third countries and dumped in the EEC at a low price,[12] and which are also based upon Commission investigations. The essential point being made here concerns a method of economic regulation which has established norms (for instance in the form of production quotas, wage levels or protective price levels), the breach of which is corrected by means of a redistributive payment. These payments may be variously termed fines or levies, but it should be understood that the element of clear disapproval connoted by use of a penal sanction is absent from or only weakly expressed in the imposition of such measures. The redistributive character of such sanctions can be appreciated from the kind of argument used by Advocate General Verloren van Themaat in his opinion in the *Queensborough Rolling Mill* case[13] when he stressed the need for equality of treatment in the imposition of fines for exceeding steel quotas:

> ... there are cogent reasons for maintaining that a system involving the imposition of fines on undertakings for exceeding their quotas that favours integrated undertakings (and at least in the case of a first infringement, leaves the undertaking with a substantial benefit) and at the same time places all specialised undertakings in respect of whose products the added value is lower at a disadvantage (as a result of its more than prohibitive effect) must also be regarded as inequitable and, in particular, as discriminatory.

Delinquency and criminality in commercial life

It is clear then that a number of different sanctions may be used to reinforce norms of economic regulation and that punitive measures constitute only one of a number of options. But even if it is accepted that a penal approach may be appropriate in some cases of economic regulation, there is the further question which arises within the realm of official penality as to how such punitive measures are themselves to be classified. A number of legal systems now distinguish between administrative and criminal offences[14] and it is this distinction which has been drawn upon in the Community system to avoid the charge that the Community has trespassed on the reserved sovereign area of Member State criminal law. Article 15(4) of Regulation 17 states categorically that the fines which may be imposed for breaches of the competition rules are not of a criminal law nature. They are thus formally described as administrative penalties and the Court of Justice has emphasised on a number of occasions, as noted in the earlier discussion, that the Commission's proceedings under Regulation 17 constitute an administrative procedure. This general concept of administrative procedure is very much a response to the needs of economic regulation. As it has become increasingly necessary to establish norms and sanctions in the field of economic, social and commercial policy, so it has been realised that the traditional repressive mechanisms of the criminal law may not be appropriate or adequate to supply the legal framework of control. They may not be appropriate because the rule-breaking which typically occurs in this context is often viewed as being qualitatively different from that which constitutes more traditional criminal offences. They may not be adequate because the personnel of criminal law enforcement may not be trained in the investigation and prosecution of 'economic' offences and the resources of the criminal law system may not be easily stretched to deal with the vast number of such breaches which are likely to occur. For such reasons, separate enforcement agencies have been established in many legal systems and sometimes a separate code of regulation and offences developed, usually based on the distinction between administrative and criminal offending.[15]

There can be little argument about the need for specialised enforcement agencies, in relation to such matters as revenue and competition. But the distinction between administrative and criminal offences is more controversial and has been less widely adopted. It is more commonly found in continental European legal systems than in common law legal systems such as those of Britain and the United States. So, among European Community states there is a divergence: the concept of administrative offence is well-established for instance in Germany and the Netherlands, but unknown in the U.K., although British practice is to talk informally of regulatory offences and to draw some practical distinctions in terms of prosecuting agencies, court jurisdiction and type of sanction (typically using fines rather than other penal measures).[16] It might be tempting to say that this divergence is little more than a descriptive difference and show that in the practice of all these systems 'economic' offences are handled differently from 'real' criminal offences and do not attract the same level of moral condemnation. Does it therefore matter whether such conduct is classified as an administrative or criminal offence?

For many purposes it is probably true to say that the distinction is semantic rather than one of huge practical import, but there is one aspect of the question where this exercise in categorisation does have significant consequences. Much of the discussion in previous chapters has centred on the level of legal protection afforded to those persons who are subject to Community investigations and sanctions and it has already been noted a number of times that the extent of this protection is sometimes alleged to depend on the nature of the offence and the procedure. That is, those subject to administrative proceedings may be entitled to a lesser degree of protection than persons who are dealt with by the criminal process. The justification for such a differential policy lies in the perceived impact of the two kinds of proceeding. Criminal proceedings can lead to the imposition of severe sanctions, including loss of liberty, and may well involve a considerable amount of social stigma. The same is said not to be true of administrative proceedings which are morally neutral and are typically backed up with pecuniary or prohibitory sanctions. One of the most stark consequences of insisting on this distinction has already been referred to in the earlier discussion, that is that administrative proceedings may not be subject to review under the European Convention on Human Rights in the same way as national criminal procedure, and the same argument has been put in relation to Community competition proceedings.[17] It has also been noted already that such arguments may not be so readily accepted by the European Court of Human Rights, as was made clear in its *Ozturk* judgement,[18] when the majority of the Court refused to follow the label given under German law but preferred to look at the substance of the issue in deciding whether the Convention should apply.

It is unlikely that much progress will be made in this discussion by seeking any further or clearer rationale for the distinction between administrative and criminal offending. A reading of the European Court of Human Rights' *Ozturk* judgement reveals the kind of impasse which has been reached in this debate. A minority of the judges did not accept that the regulatory or administrative character of road traffic offences under German law should so easily be re-categorised as criminal for Convention purposes. Yet at the same time their arguments amounted in the end to little more than a defence of the legislative policy of decriminalisation which the majority of the Court was in any case ready enough to approve as serving the interests of both the individual and the needs of the proper administration of justice.[19] It has to be accepted that the dichotomy is adopted in some legal systems but not in others, and that there is little incentive for, or expectation of, harmonisation in this area. The important question to be decided is rather that of whether the distinction should have any bearing on the extent of legal protection and to do this it may be useful to move on from the concepts of 'criminality', and 'criminal' and 'administrative' sanctions to a more broadly based analysis of 'delinquency' and 'repressive' measures.

A widespread ambivalence towards the use of criminal law as an instrument of economic regulation – such as is found for instance in the field of competition policy – should not distract discussion from the essential need to recognise certain forms of delinquent behaviour in the commercial world. Yet, such is the complexity of much economic activity that it may take some time for such delinquent behaviour to emerge as such. There is now no doubt as to the delinquent character of fraud, since the clear element of dishonesty attracts a wide measure of moral opprobrium. But practices such as insider dealing and share support activities have only recently been categorised as criminal acts and the cost-effectiveness of criminal proceedings to deal with such behaviour and the appropriate level of sanctions remains a subject of argument.[20] Anti-competitive practices present a similar quandary. Although they are now subject to a near universal condemnation in industrialised countries, the strength of that condemnation is still variable and, as much of the above discussion has demonstrated, the best mechanisms for its control are still being formulated. This state of play at the present stage of regulating anti-competitive conduct therefore requires a cautionary approach towards the adoption of criminal law techniques. Unless a convincing argument may be put forward that breaches of the competition rules may be equated in moral terms with fraud and other forms of dishonest economic transaction, criminal proceedings are unlikely to command wide support in this area.

On the other hand, there should be a clearly expressed official recognition of the damaging outcome of some restrictive practices and the real element of delinquency on the part of those undertakings who repeatedly infringe the competition rules in full knowledge of what they are doing. There is no inconsistency in describing such behaviour as delinquent, in the sense that it is strongly disapproved of and considered fit for strict regulation, while not imposing criminal liability. To insist on labelling such conduct as criminal runs the risk of making the public interest hostage to the difficulties and disadvantages of using criminal law – those factors that have prompted moves towards decriminalisation in legal systems such as that of Germany. On the other hand, the looser, though no less morally hard-hitting label of 'delinquency' justifies intervention while leaving the way clear for a flexible response. It is the imperative and retributive character of criminal law – in which the strength of the condemnation suggests a moral obligation to respond officially and impose sanctions – that gives rise to an inherent weakness of inflexibility, rendering it sometimes a heavy-handed and blunt instrument of control. This fact has long been recognised in some contexts, such as health and safety at work in Britain, in respect of which a legislative move was made in the 1970s away from reliance on criminal sanctions.[21] Yet in the traditional area of criminal law, informal and flexible responses are still viewed with some suspicion: negotiated settlement of criminal cases (such as compounding) may be criticised as compromising a prosecutorial imperative, while measures such as cautioning and reparation may be seen by some as 'going soft' on criminality.

But it is clear that in the area of economic regulation, and in particular that of competition policy, a flexible response is appropriate in both moral and practical terms. Not all restrictions of competition can be categorically condemned, nor are the resources ever going to be available for a wide-ranging process of investigation and formal decision. The experience of the Commission in the field of competition policy in the EEC provides a very clear case-study to this effect. It has been seen how, for practical reasons, the Commission had necessarily to concentrate its resources of formal investigation and decision on a small proportion of the most serious cases, at the same time developing informal and bureaucratic mechanisms for resolving expeditiously the vast number of less problematical restrictions. This bifurcated approach left the greater part of the field to be dealt with by means of negotiated approval, while true delinquency in anti-competitive behaviour was identified and subjected to a repressive, and increasingly in some cases, a penal response. In the discussion in earlier chapters such delinquent conduct has sometimes been referred to as comprising an antitrust offence, a term which implies neither criminality nor administrative offence. That latter categorisation has perforce been adopted by the Community authorities, but the analogy with some national systems of administrative procedure has not proven ultimately very helpful. The essential point to note is that one option available to deal with breaches of the EEC competition rules has been to employ *repressive* sanctions, and it is the consequences of that fact which need to be discussed.

Repressive sanctions and legal protection

It is noticeable that in much of its comparative legal analysis both the Court of Justice and its Advocates General have sometimes had to skirt around analogical distinctions drawn from national legal systems, such as those between criminal and administrative procedures and between corporate and natural persons. In some cases, these distinctions were productive of disarray ('a mosaic of national approaches', in the words of Advocate General Darmon),[22] evidencing a divergence of approach as between Member State legal systems and no doubt privately convincing the Court that it might just as well start afresh. There was a significant moment in this respect in the Court's *Orkem* judgement[23] when it had to decide on an undertaking's right not to incriminate itself. Whereas Advocate General Darmon in that case was persuaded that a right to silence was confined to criminal proceedings – he was also unwilling to build upon the reasoning of the majority of the European Court of Human Rights in *Ozturk* – the Court of Justice broke away from the national examples. The guiding principle, in the Court's view, was the fairness of the proceedings, however labelled, and this required that the undertaking's ability to defend itself effectively at the hearing should not be irrevocably undermined at the time of the investigation. This argument clearly gives priority to the substantive character of the proceedings and that is used to determine what is necessary in terms of rights of defence, rather than a formal description derived from another context.

Much of the procedure used by the Commission in the field of competition policy is informal and bureaucratic, leading to a negotiated outcome in individual cases rather than the application of formal sanctions. In that context, rights of defence do not assume such a crucial aspect. But in those minority of serious cases, where extensive powers of investigation are used and in which there is a possibility of intrusive and highly publicised sanctions, such rights are essential to guarantee fair process. It is doubtful whether it helps very much in legal argument simply to assert that these proceedings are similar to criminal proceedings at a national level. That is partly true, but partly not true. But in terms of their substantive character, formal competition proceedings are legally significant and deal with serious matters. It would certainly be misleading to compare them with proceedings to deal with a minor road traffic offence (as in *Ozturk*), which the analogy of 'administrative offence' might suggest. The formal procedure under Regulation 17 is used selectively to deal with alleged infringements which are of economic significance and amount to a blatant disregard of established rules, and constitute an important economic injury to other traders and consumers. This is a matter far removed from the 'minor' offence which German law has sought to decriminalise. Concomitantly, involvement in such proceedings is a serious matter, since the undertakings concerned are subject to far-reaching powers of investigation and potentially severe sanctions. If, on the one hand, the analogy of criminal proceedings is not appropriate, nor is that of administrative procedure, as it is commonly applied at the national level.

Enough has been said already to indicate the incursive nature of Commission investigations in this area. It remains to emphasise the broadly repressive character of the sanctions which may be applied under Regulation 17. Both the orders to desist or carry out positive action and the pecuniary sanctions are of a clearly coercive character and the punitive objective of the fines has been confirmed a number of times by the Court of Justice. In contrast to the solutions arrived at in the non-contentious area of competition law enforcement, these are formal dispositions made in the knowledge that these cases cannot be resolved by amicable negotiation but are situations in which it is necessary to resort to measures of prevention and condemnation. It is in relation to the sanctions that may be used in these proceedings that there appears to be the closest analogy to the national concept of a criminal proceeding. They follow upon a formal and public determination that the party in question is in breach of the rules (rather like a conviction) and the range of sanctions displays the retributive, deterrent and preventive concerns of criminal law sentencing. Moreover, such measures contain a strong element of disapproval and moral condemnation since they relate to conduct which is significantly injurious and consciously flouts established norms. It is therefore what may be described as the *repressive* character of formal competition proceedings which justifies the extensive structure of legal protection that has now been developed and may be regarded as essential for the purpose of ensuring fair treatment of those subject to such proceedings.

The element of supranational control

It is both a distinctive and a complicating feature of the Commission's competition procedure that it represents a departure from the tradition of national control of the behaviour of individuals and undertakings. Apart from exceptional instances, such as the international trial of war criminals following the end of war in 1945, even when conduct has been condemned at the international level, enforcement of that condemnation has in practice been delegated to national courts and authorities.[24] The Commission's investigatory role and powers of enforcement therefore stand as a radical development in the field of the legal control of delinquency, but it may be asked to what extent this is a special case rather than a model for the future: has it set a precedent for the further transfer of such powers to either the European Community or other supranational authorities, or is it likely to remain a singular development?

It may be instructive to compare these developments in the field of competition policy with other situations in the context of the European Community where some arguments have been put forward for similar powers to be transferred to the supranational level. One special problem has been the control of fraudulent dealings in Community funds, particularly in the area of agricultural policy, where a complex system of levies, subsidies, refunds and other payments provide ample opportunity for fraudulent exploitation.[25] Such frauds are likely to amount to criminal offences under national law and so at first sight could adequately be dealt with at that level. However, problems of investigation, of expertise on the part of the national agencies of enforcement and of motivation – to deal with transactions which injure the Community rather than the national interest – have combined to render action at the national level patchy and in many cases ineffective. Differences in criminal law definitions, evidential rules and enforcement policy as between Member States have compounded the problem. The Commission is able to undertake a supervisory role and this has been developed considerably in recent years,[26] but is unable to take direct action itself in relation to a problem which affects the Community interest rather than that of Member States. One possible solution would be for the Commission to be given similar powers of investigation and enforcement to those that it has already in the field of competition, so that rather than coordinating national enforcement at a distance, it can use its own expertise and incentive to take action to establish a system of direct legal control.[27]

The objections to, and problems with such a development are, however, familiar. It has been seen already that national governments are sensitive about the transfer of criminal law powers to the Community: this is a sensitive area reserved, in political if not legal terms, to state sovereignty.[28] If powers were transferred, as has happened in the field of competition, as an administrative competence, this would lead to a situation in which conduct of a clearly criminal nature according to national law would be proceeded against as an administrative offence at the Community level. Just as important are the practical difficulties which are likely to be encountered. Such a move would necessarily entail a massive transfer of resources to the Community in terms of personnel and facilities, if the Commission is to go beyond a highly selective policy of enforcement. While such a selective approach may be justifiable in the context of competition infringements, it would not be at all easily justified as regards frauds against the Community, where what is involved is a large number of serious and damaging transactions which already qualify as serious criminal offences under national law. In short, for a mixture of reasons of principle and practicality, such a development is unlikely to come about.

One further point can be made, which emphasises the distinctive character of the developments in the enforcement of competition policy. In the case of frauds against the Community, and of many other types of conduct where the impetus for control comes from the Community, such as environmental damage or the management of fishing stocks, the enforcement can in principle be carried out appropriately at the national level. Criminal or administrative offences may already exist, or can be introduced with little effort and the Community's role may be restricted to the harmonisation of these national efforts throughout the Community. The same is not true of Community competition policy. Although restrictive practices and cartels are also controlled at the national level, the purpose and scope of that control is different. Community policy is concerned with the Community dimension of anti-competitive behaviour, which may be significantly different in terms of its appreciation and analysis and, as discussed in Chapter 9, this presents problems for the delegation of enforcement of Community policy to the national level. In other words, there may be said to be a specifically supranational element in the Community's competition rules, which both justifies and necessitates a supranational mode of enforcement.

This suggests therefore that the experiment in supranational control which has been discussed here is of a special kind. While it arises from the exigencies of giving effect to competition policy at a supranational level, it may not be a suitable or necessary model for other contexts. It has been a necessary departure from the traditional method of legal control, and will continue to develop as such, but like the Community legal system itself, it may come to be regarded as a system of control *sui generis*.[29]

Notes

1 See, for example, John Stuart Mill, *On Liberty* (1859); cf. Nicola Lacey, *State Punishment* (1988, Routledge), Ch. 5.
2 For the earlier attitude of the criminal law in relation to fraud, see the comments of Chief Justice Holt in *Jones* (1704) 2 Ld Raym 1013: 'Shall we indict one man for making a fool of another?'
3 For a useful recent overview and critique of arguments concerning penal abolition and moves away from the criminal sanction, see Willem de Haan, *The Politics of Redress* (1990, Unwin Hyman).
4 Regulation 1017/68, J.O. 1968, L175/1 (road, rail and inland waterways), closely modelled on Articles 85 and 86 and Regulation 17/62; Regulation 4056/86, O.J. 1986, L378/4 (sea transport).
5 See Christopher Bellamy and Graham Child, *Common Market Law of Competition* (3rd ed., 1987, Sweet & Maxwell), p. 604 *et seq.*
6 See generally the discussion of punishment in Christopher Harding and Richard W. Ireland, *Punishment: Rhetoric, Rule and Practice* (1989, Routledge).
7 See Bellamy and Child, op. cit., p. 592 *et seq.*
8 Decision 3485/85, O.J. 1985, L340/5, Article 12.
9 See Decision 379/84, O.J. 1984, L46/23.
10 Case 64/84, *Queensborough Rolling Mills v Commission* (1986) 2 C.M.L.R. 211 (this reviews a number of the cases on quota production fines).
11 For an example see the Commission's *Tenth Report on Competition Policy* (1980), point 109 (a fine of 900,000 ECU imposed on a number of French and German undertakings).
12 See Bellamy and Child, op. cit., pp. 604–11.
13 Case 64/84, *Queensborough Rolling Mills v Commission* (1986) 2 C.M.L.R., at p. 213.
14 For an overview of the concept of the administrative offence, especially in German law, see the judgement of the European Court of Human Rights in *Ozturk v Germany* (1984) E.H.R.Rep. 409, p. 412 *et seq.*
15 The German model is perhaps one of the most well developed. For an earlier account, see John H. Langbein, 'Controlling Prosecutorial Discretion in Germany' 41 (1973) *University of Chicago Law Review*, 439. German law distinguishes between *Straftat* (a criminal offence) and *Ordnungswidrigkeit* (a regulatory or administrative offence).
16 In fact, much of the jurisdiction of magistrates' courts in England and Wales is concerned with such 'regulatory' offences.
17 See, for example, Advocate General Darmon in Case 374/87, *Orkem v Commission* (1989) E.C.R. 3318.
18 See note 14 above.
19 (1984) E.H.R.Rep., pp. 420–1.
20 See, for instance, some of the discussion by Michael Levi, 'Sentencing White-Collar Crime in the Dark? Reflections on the Guinness Four', 30 (1991) *Howard Journal of Criminal Justice* 257: '... whatever the jury ... might have thought, the Guinness share support operation was on the borderline of criminality and of accepted conduct among commercial people at the time' (p. 276).
21 Health and Safety at Work Act 1974, based on the recommendations of the *Report of the Committee on Safety and Health at Work*, Cmnd 5034 (1972).

22 (1989) E.C.R., p. 3332.
23 See note 17 above.
24 As is the case with the trial of the great majority of war criminals and others, e.g. pirates, who have been prosecuted for crimes under international law.
25 For a general account of the problem, see Ann Sherlock and Christopher Harding, 'Controlling Fraud within the European Community', 16 (1991) E.L.Rev. 20; House of Lords Select Committee on the European Communities, *Fraud Against the Community*, H.L. 27, February 21, 1989.
26 See Regulation 4045/89, O.J. 1989, L388/18.
27 As recommended, for example, by Tiedemann: see House of Lords Select Committee Report, op. cit., para. 124, QQ 294 *et seq*; see also Sherlock and Harding, op. cit., pp. 34–5.
28 Sherlock and Harding, op. cit., p. 32.
29 The term used by the Court of Justice in Case 26/62, *Van Gend en Loos v Nederlandse Tariefcommissie* (1963) E.C.R. 1.

Bibliography

Baldwin, J. R., 'Pre-Trial Settlement in Magistrates' Courts', 24 (1985) *Howard Journal of Criminal Justice*, 108.

Bellamy, Christopher and Child, Graham, *Common Market Law of Competition*, (3rd ed., 1987, Sweet & Maxwell).

Braithwaite, John, *Corporate Crime in the Pharmaceutical Industry* (1984, Routledge and Kegan Paul).

Braun, Antoine, 'Les Droits de la Defense devant la Commission et la Cour de Justice des Communautés européenes', 2 – 1980 *Revue Internationale de la Concurrence*, 2.

Brown, L. Neville and Garner, J. F., *French Administrative Law* (4th ed., 1983, Butterworths).

Brownlie, Ian, *Principles of Public International Law* (3rd ed., 1990, Oxford University Press).

Burnside, Alec and Stuart, Eugene, 'Irish Competition Law – Moving Towards the European Model', 13 (1992) E.C.L.R. 38.

Commission of the European Communities, *Report on Competition Policy*, published annually by the Office for Official Publications of the European Communities, Luxembourg.

Council of Europe, European Committee on Crime Problems, *Economic Crime* (1981).

Davidson, Joel, 'EEC Fact-Finding Procedures in Competition Cases: An American Critique', 14 (1977) C.M.L.Rev. 175.

de Haan, Willem, *The Politics of Redress* (1990, Unwin Hyman).

Delmas-Marty, M and Roche-Pire, E., *Marché Commun et Criminalités des Affaires* (1982, Economica).

Deringer, Arved, 'The Distribution of Powers in the Enforcement of the Rules of Competition under the Rome Treaty', 1 (1963-64) C.M.L.Rev. 30.

Edwards, Corwin D., *Control of Cartels and Monopolies: An International Comparison* (1967, Oceana).

Edwards, D. A. O., *The Professional Secret, Confidentiality, and Legal Professional Privilege in the Nine Member States of the European Community* (1975, CCBE).

Faull, Jonathan, 'Legal Professional Privilege (AM&S): The Commission Proposes International Negotiations', 10 (1985) E.L.Rev. 119.

Ferry, J., 'Procedures and Powers of the EEC Commission in Antitrust Cases', (1979) *European Intellectual Property Review*, 126.

Forrester, Ian and Norall, Christopher, 'The Laicisation of Community Law: Self-Help and the Rule of Reason: How Competition Law Is and Could Be Applied', 21 (1984) C.M.L.Rev. 11.

Galanter, M., 'Judicial Mediation in the United States', 12 (1985) *Journal of Law and Society*, 1.

Goyder, D. G., *EEC Competition Law* (1988, Oxford University Press).

Graupner, Frances, 'Commission Decision-Making on Competition Questions', 10 (1973) C.M.L.Rev. 291.

Harding, Christopher and Ireland, Richard W., *Punishment: Rhetoric, Rule and Practice* (1989, Routledge).

Hartley, T. C., *The Foundations of European Community Law* (2nd ed., 1988, Oxford University Press).

Hay, Peter, 'The Federal Jurisdiction of the Common Market Court', 12 (1963) *American Journal of Comparative Law*, 39.

Joshua, J. M., 'The Element of Surprise: EEC Competition Investigations under Article 14(3) of Regulation 17', 17 (1983) E.L.Rev. 3.

— 'Proof in Contested EEC Competition Cases: A Comparison with the Rules of Evidence in Common Law', 12 (1987) E.L.Rev. 315.

Kaysen, C. and Turner, D. F., *Antitrust Policy* (1959, Harvard University Press).

Kerse, C. S., *EEC Antitrust Procedure* (2nd ed. 1987, 1st ed. 1981, European Law Centre).

Korah, Valentine, 'The Rights of the Defence in Administrative Proceedings under Community Law', 33 (1980) *Current Legal Problems*, 73.

— *An Introductory Guide to EEC Competition Law and Practice* (4th ed., 1990, ESC Publishing).

Kuyper, P. J. and van Rijn, T. P. J. N., 'Procedural Guarantees and Investigatory Methods, with Special Reference to Competition', 2 (1982) *Yearbook of European Law*, 1.

Lacey, Nicola, *State Punishment* (1988, Routledge).

Lang, John Temple, 'The Procedure of the Commission in Competition Cases', 14 (1977) C.M.L.Rev. 155.

— 'The Position of Third Parties in EEC Competition Cases', 3 (1978) E.L.Rev. 177.

— 'The Power of the Commission to Order Interim Measures in Competition Cases', 18 (1981) C.M.L.Rev. 49.

Langbein, John H., 'Controlling Prosecutorial Discretion in Germany', 41 (1973) *University of Chicago Law Review*, 439.

Lasok, D. and Bridge, J. W., *Law and Institutions of the European Communities* (5th ed., 1991, Butterworths).

Lasok, K. P. E., 'Procedure in Anti-dumping Investigations', 8 (1987) E.C.L.R.

Lavoie, Chantal, 'The Investigation Powers of the Commission with Respect to Business Secrets under Community Competition Rules', 17 (1992) E.L.Rev. 20.

Levi, Michael, *Regulating Fraud: White Collar Crime and the Criminal Process* (1987, Tavistock).

— 'Developments in Business Crime in Europe', Chapter 12 in Frances Heidensohn and Martin Farrell (eds), *Crime in Europe* (1991, Routledge).

— 'Sentencing White-Collar Crime in the Dark? Reflections on the Guiness Four', 30 (1991) *Howard Journal of Criminal Justice*, 257.

Mancini, Alessandra, 'The Italian Law in Defence of Competition and the Market', 12 (1991) E.C.L.R. 45.

March Hunnings, Neville, 'The Stanley Adams Affair or The Biter Bit', 24 (1987) C.M.L.Rev. 65.

Mill, John Stuart, *On Liberty* (1859).

Passas, Nikos and Nelken, David, 'The Legal Responses to Agricultural Fraud in the European Community' (1991, unpublished paper).

Pliakos, Asteris, *Les droits de la défense et le droit communautaire de la concurrence* (1987, Bruylant).

Posner, Richard, *Antitrust Law: An Economic Perspective*, (1976, University of Chicago Press).

Pritchett, C. Herman, *Constitutional Civil Liberties* (1984, Prentice-Hall).

Rubio de Casas, Maria G., 'The Spanish Law for the Defence of Competition', 11 (1990) E.C.L.R. 179.

Shapiro, S., *Wayward Capitalists* (1983, Yale University Press).

Sherlock, Ann and Harding, Christopher, 'Controlling Fraud within the European Community', 16 (1991) E.L.Rev. 20.

Smith, Paul, 'The Wolf in Wolf's Clothing: The Problem with Predatory Pricing', 14 (1989) E.L.Rev. 209.

Svernlov, Carl and Gustafsson, Leif, 'Stricter Anti-trust Enforcement in Sweden', 12 (1991) E.C.L.R. 245.

Thiesing, Schroter and Hochbaum, *Les ententes et les positions dominantes dans le droit de la CEE* (1977, Jupiter, ed. Navarre).

Van Bael, Ivo, 'EEC Anti-Trust Enforcement and Adjudication as seen by Defence Counsel', 7 (1979) *Revue Suisse de Droit International de la Concurrence*, 1.

— 'Comment on the EEC Commission's Antitrust Settlement Practice: The Shortcircuiting of Regulation 17?', 22 (1984) *Swiss Review of International Competition Law*, 67.

Van der Ersch, B., 'Due Process in the Administrative Application of the European Community's Competition Rules', 2 – 1980, *Revue Internationale de la Concurrence*, 9.

Whish, Richard, *Competition Law* (2nd ed., 1989, Butterworths).

Wyatt, Derek, 'New Legal Order or Old?', 7 (1982) E.L.Rev. 147.

Index

Abuse of a dominant position 77, 85, 88,
    105–109
Adams, Stanley 15, 58–59
Administrative procedure, concept of 2,
    7–8, 22–23, 43, 61–62, 76–77,
    35–138
Advisory Committee on
    Restrictive Practices and Monopolies
    48–49, 72
Aniline Dyes Cartel,
    see Dyestuffs Cartel
Anti-dumping procedure 63, 131
Antitrust awareness, concept of 85 et
    seq, 105, 106, 109, 110–111
Antitrust delinquency, concept of 98 et
    seq

Business secrets 50, 54–57

Cartel activities 86, 97–104
Cautioning, in criminal procedure 68
Cease and desist order 79
Civil remedies, under Member State law
    115–118
Comfort letters 71–72, 86
Commission,
    DG 1V 11–12, 43–44
    legal service 12–13
    rapporteur 12–13, 47
    resources of 11, 68, 70 et seq
    sector enquiries by 15–16
Compliance programmes 76
Compounding 69–70
Concerted practice 101
Confidentiality 15, 50, 54 et seq

between lawyer and client 28–31
    see also Business secrets
Corporate persons, legal protection of
    23, 32
Criminal sanctions 6–8, 22–23, 77, 79 et
    seq, 130 et seq
Crisis cartels 77, 99
Customs fraud 69–70

Damages,
    for competitive injury 115–118
    for disclosure of identity 58–59
Dawn raid,
    see Surprise inspection
Defence, rights of 41 et seq
Deringer Committee Report 27, 34–35
Deterrence, in fining practice 82, 88,
    91–92
Direct effect 4, 115
Discriminatory pricing 108
Divestiture of companies 80
Dyestuffs Cartel 87, 100 et seq, 121,
    124–125

European Atomic Energy Community
    37
European Coal and Steel Community 3,
    4, 33, 60–61, 122, 131–134
    fines under 132–134
European Convention on Human
    Rights 7, 13, 22, 27, 29, 32, 33, 43,
    136
European Parliament 13, 44, 73
Exemplary punishment 90
Export bans 54, 85, 88, 92, 104–105

Export deterrents 105

Fines 47, 75, 81 *et seq*, 125
    effect of 91–93
    punitive character 82 *et seq*
'Fishing expedition' 16–17, 26
Forcible entry 34–37, 119–120
Forcible seizure,
    see Inspection
France, administrative law 12
    competition law 70
Fraud, compared to anti-competitive
    behaviour 52, 130
    in relation to Community funds
    140–141

Germany, competition law 35, 37–38,
    70, 100, 106, 120, 124
Group exemptions 86, 115

Hearing 41–50
    and third parties 61–62
Hearing Officer 41, 44, 48
Hoechst 19, 31–32, 36–37, 87, 93, 100,
    102–103, 119, 121
Hoffmann-la Roche 15, 57, 58, 85, 107

Informal settlement 46, 61–62, 64, 68 *et
    seq*, 92–93
    criticisms of 92–93
Informants, protection of 57–59
Information, requests for by
    Commission 16–17, 24 *et seq*
Injury, caused by anti-competitive acts
    87–88
Inspection, by Commission 17–20, 24
Intentional breach of competition rules
    83–86
Interim protection 59–61
International Atomic Energy Agency 5
International Covenant on Civil and
    Political Rights 27
Investigation, by Commission 11–40
    see also Inspection
Italy, competition law 38

Japan, competition law penalties 82
Judicial review 15, 22, 30, 42, 56, 62–65,
    72

Judicial warrant 34–37
Jurisdiction, extra-territorial 123–126
    overlapping 120–123

Legal professional privilege,
    see Confidentiality
Legal representation 34, 38–39, 48
Levy, concept of 132 *et seq*
Loyalty rebates 107

Market sharing 99–104

National agencies, cooperation with
    Commission 18–20, 34 *et seq*,
    118–120
    enforcement by 3–4, 11, 114–118, 120
Negative clearance 14
Negligent breach of competition rules
    83, 86
Norway, competition law 81–82
Notification 6, 13–14, 70–71, 86, 101

Offence, concept of in competition
    proceedings 82 *et seq*, 98 *et seq*
Opening of proceedings by Commission
    41–43
Oral explanations 33–34
Oral hearings 47–48

Periodic penalty payments 93, 120
Plea bargaining 74–76, 87
Polypropylene Cartel 87, 91, 94–95,
    102–104
Predatory pricing 107–108, 109
Price fixing 85, 88, 99–104
Pricing policy, orders in relation to 80
Private premises, inviolability of 31–32
Procedural infringements 82, 93
Proportionality, principle of 15–16,
    25–26
PVC Cartel 1, 31, 102–104
Publication, of Commission's decisions
    49, 72

Quinine Cartel 84, 94, 100 *et seq*,
    122–123

Recidivist behaviour 86–87, 90, 102–103

Refusal to supply 54, 60, 79–80, 101,
    106–107, 109

Scales, of fines 88–91
Search, concept of 19, 24, 37–38
    see also Inspection
Selective distribution 52, 54, 61, 63
Self-incrimination 26–28
State aids 63–64
Statement of objections 44–46
Successor undertakings, liability of
    94–95
Sugar Cartel 101, 107
Supranational control, concept of 3–5
Surprise inspections 32–34
Switzerland, espionage law 15, 58
    reaction to extra-territorial
    jurisdiction 125–126

Tax fraud 69–70

Termination of infringements, orders
    79–81
Thermoplastics industry,
    investigation of 1, 17, 26
Third parties, complaints by 13–16,
    53–54
    and judicial review 62–65
    rights of 47, 52 *et seq*, 118
Time limits 42, 94
Trade unions, rights of complaint 54
Transport, regulation of 4
Turnover, in calculation of fines 88–91

Unfair pricing 108–109
United States, antitrust law 6, 11, 70, 81,
    100, 116, 122–123, 124
    imprisonment, for antitrust
    violations 81